Hans Mol

English for

TOURISM AND HOSPITALITY

in Higher Education Studies

Course Book

Series editor: Terry Phillips

Published by
Garnet Publishing Ltd.
8 Southern Court
South Street
Reading RG1 4QS, UK

First published 2008
Reprinted 2008

ISBN 978 1 85964 942 8

British Cataloguing-in-Publication Data
A catalogue record for this book is available from the British Library.

Production
Series editor: Terry Phillips
Lead authors: Carolyn Walker, Marian Dunn
Project management: Louise Elkins, Martin Moore
Editorial team: Jane Gregory, Rebecca Snelling
Academic review: Frances Devine
Design: Henry Design Associates and Mike Hinks
Photography: Sally Henry and Trevor Cook; Alamy (Mike Goldwater); Clipart.com; Corbis (Bobby Yip); Getty Images (Eightfish, Yellow Dog Productions)

Audio recorded at Motivation Sound Studios produced by EFS Television Production Ltd.

The author and publisher would like to thank the following for permission to reproduce from copyright material:
Times online for page 17 article adapted from *Time to go backpacking in style* by Stephen Bleach and Brian Schofield
The Guardian for page 19 article adapted from *Is it as green as it's painted?* by Esther Addley
Google for results listings on page 35

Every effort has been made to trace copyright holders and we apologize in advance for any unintentional omission. We will be happy to insert the appropriate acknowledgements in any subsequent editions.

Printed and bound in Lebanon by International Press

Author's acknowledgement

English for Tourism and Hospitality is, first and foremost, an English language course for students studying the subject. In my teaching career I have had extensive experience with students studying (international) business and tourism-related subjects but I could not have written the course without the help of others.

I would like to express my sincerest thanks to Drs Mieke Witsel MA MACE FRSA, of Southern Cross University's School of Tourism and Hospitality Management, Lismore, New South Wales, Australia, who has been my industry education support during the writing, and who supplied the basis for a number of the lectures in the units focusing on listening skills. She also tirelessly suggested relevant and new literature and sources for the reading components. Many thanks, Mieke – without your input this publication would have been a different thing altogether.

In the writing of *English for Tourism and Hospitality*, I have consulted the literature and attempted to select the most prominent, relevant and current exponents of research in tourism and hospitality. I can only modestly hope that I've quoted them appropriately, paid tribute to their achievements and correctly interpreted their visions and findings.

Hans Mol

Introduction

English for Tourism and Hospitality is designed for students who plan to take a course in the area of tourism and/or hospitality entirely or partly in English. The principal aim of *English for Tourism and Hospitality* is to teach students to cope with input texts, i.e., listening and reading, in the discipline. However, students will be expected to produce output texts in speech and writing throughout the course.

The syllabus focuses on key vocabulary for the discipline and on words and phrases commonly used in academic and technical English. It covers key facts and concepts from the discipline, thereby giving students a flying start for when they meet the same points again in their faculty work. It also focuses on the skills that will enable students to get the most out of lectures and written texts. Finally, it presents the skills required to take part in seminars and tutorials and to produce essay assignments.

English for Tourism and Hospitality comprises:

- this student Course Book, including audio transcripts and wordlist
- the Teacher's Book, which provides detailed guidance on each lesson, full answer keys, audio transcripts and extra photocopiable resources
- audio CDs with lecture and seminar excerpts

English for Tourism and Hospitality has 12 units, each of which is based on a different aspect of tourism or hospitality. Odd-numbered units are based on listening (lecture/seminar extracts). Even-numbered units are based on reading.

Each unit is divided into four lessons:

Lesson 1: vocabulary for the discipline; vocabulary skills such as word-building, use of affixes, use of synonyms for paraphrasing

Lesson 2: reading or listening text and skills development

Lesson 3: reading or listening skills extension. In addition, in later reading units, students are introduced to a writing assignment which is further developed in Lesson 4; in later listening units, students are introduced to a spoken language point (e.g., making an oral presentation at a seminar) which is further developed in Lesson 4

Lesson 4: a parallel listening or reading text to that presented in Lesson 2 which students have to use their new skills (Lesson 3) to decode; in addition, written or spoken work is further practised

The last two pages of each unit, *Vocabulary bank* and *Skills bank*, are a useful summary of the unit content.

Each unit provides between 4 and 6 hours of classroom activity with the possibility of a further 2-4 hours on the suggested extra activities. The course will be suitable, therefore, as the core component of a faculty-specific pre-sessional or foundation course of between 50 and 80 hours.

It is assumed that prior to using this book students will already have completed a general EAP (English for Academic Purposes) course such as *Skills in English* (Garnet Publishing, up to the end at least of Level 3), and will have achieved an IELTS level of at least 5.

For a list of other titles in this series, see www.garneteducation.com/

Book map

Vocabulary focus	Skills focus		Unit
• words from general English with a special meaning in tourism • prefixes and suffixes	**Listening**	• preparing for a lecture • predicting lecture content from the introduction • understanding lecture organization • choosing an appropriate form of notes • making lecture notes	**1**
	Speaking	• speaking from notes	
• English–English dictionaries: headwords · definitions · parts of speech · phonemes · stress markers · countable/uncountable · transitive/intransitive	**Reading**	• using research questions to focus on relevant information in a text • using topic sentences to get an overview of the text	**2**
	Writing	• writing topic sentences • summarizing a text	
• stress patterns in multi-syllable words • hospitality outlets	**Listening**	• preparing for a lecture • predicting lecture content • making lecture notes • using different information sources	**3**
	Speaking	• reporting research findings • formulating questions	
• computer jargon • abbreviations and acronyms • job titles • discourse and stance markers • verb and noun suffixes	**Reading**	• identifying topic development within a paragraph • using the Internet effectively • evaluating Internet search results	**4**
	Writing	• reporting research findings	
• word sets: synonyms, antonyms, etc. • the language of trends • common lecture language	**Listening**	• understanding 'signpost language' in lectures • using symbols and abbreviations in note-taking	**5**
	Speaking	• making effective contributions to a seminar	
• synonyms, replacement subjects, etc. for sentence-level paraphrasing	**Reading**	• locating key information in complex sentences	**6**
	Writing	• writing complex sentences • reporting findings from other sources: paraphrasing	
• compound nouns • fixed phrases from tourism • fixed phrases from academic English • common lecture language	**Listening**	• understanding speaker emphasis	**7**
	Speaking	• asking for clarification • responding to queries and requests for clarification	
• synonyms • nouns from verbs • definitions • common 'direction' verbs in essay titles (*discuss, analyse, evaluate,* etc.)	**Reading**	• understanding dependent clauses with passives	**8**
	Writing	• paraphrasing • expanding notes into complex sentences • recognizing different essay types/structures: descriptive · analytical · comparison/evaluation · argument • writing essay plans • writing essays	
• fixed phrases from tourism • fixed phrases from academic English	**Listening**	• using the Cornell note-taking system • recognizing digressions in lectures	**9**
	Speaking	• making effective contributions to a seminar • referring to other people's ideas in a seminar	
• 'neutral' and 'marked' words • job titles (management/supervisory) • fixed phrases from management • fixed phrases from academic English	**Reading**	• recognizing the writer's stance and level of confidence or tentativeness • inferring implicit ideas	**10**
	Writing	• writing situation–problem–solution–evaluation essays • using direct quotations • compiling a bibliography/reference list	
• words/phrases used to link ideas (*moreover, as a result,* etc.) • stress patterns in noun phrases and compounds • fixed phrases from academic English • words/phrases related to environmental issues	**Listening**	• recognizing the speaker's stance • writing up notes in full	**11**
	Speaking	• building an argument in a seminar • agreeing/disagreeing	
• verbs used to introduce ideas from other sources (*X contends/accepts/asserts that* …) • linking words/phrases conveying contrast (*whereas*), result (*consequently*), reasons (*due to*), etc. • words for quantities (*a significant minority*)	**Reading**	• understanding how ideas in a text are linked	**12**
	Writing	• deciding whether to use direct quotation or paraphrase • incorporating quotations • writing research reports • writing effective introductions/conclusions	

1 WHAT IS TOURISM?

A Read the text. The red words are probably familiar to you in general English. But can you think of a different meaning for each word in tourism?

> It was nearly 9.00. The letter should come today with news of her promotion. Head of the Africa office! She checked in the hall again, but there was still nothing. Suddenly, there was a ring at the front door. It must be the postman! But why had he rung the bell? Jane opened the door. The postman was holding a package, not a letter. Of course! It was the book she had ordered. At least she could stay in, relax in her armchair and read about Africa today.

B Complete each sentence with one of the red words from Exercise A. Change the form if necessary (e.g., change a noun into an adjective).

1 Who did you ＿＿＿＿＿＿＿ your tickets with?

2 Have you seen the new ＿＿＿＿＿＿＿ literature for World Break Holidays?

3 Many return airline fares are cheaper for periods which include a Saturday night ＿＿＿＿＿＿＿ .

4 Do you want a ＿＿＿＿＿＿＿ holiday or do you want to arrange accommodation and car hire separately?

5 He's just an ＿＿＿＿＿＿＿ tourist. He never actually goes anywhere.

6 Which counter do we ＿＿＿＿＿＿＿ in for Flight EK 004?

C Study the words in box a.

1 What is the connection between all the words?

2 What is the base word in each case?

3 What do we call the extra letters?

4 What is the meaning of each prefix?

5 Can you think of another word with each prefix?

> **a**
> dissatisfaction   intangible
> international   multinational   overbook
> reconfirm   transport   underpay

D Study the words in box b.

1 What is the connection between all the words?

2 What is the base word in each case?

3 What do we call the extra letters?

4 What effect do the extra letters have on the base word?

5 Can you think of another word with each suffix?

> **b**
> advertisement   broaden
> direction   hospitality   promotional
> stressful   tourism

E Discuss the illustrations on the opposite page using words from this page where possible.

1

$$CS = D - E$$

customer satisfaction   delivery   expectation

2

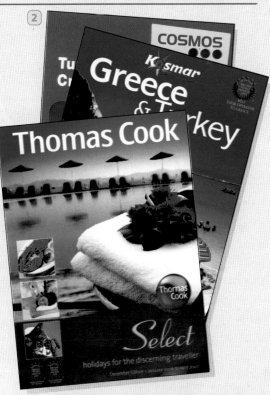

COSMOS

Kosmar **Greece & Turkey**

Thomas Cook

Select

holidays for the discerning traveller

3

SRI LANKA from **£699**

7 nights **all inclusive** at a fabulous beach resort
Included in the price:
- return scheduled flights from the UK
- all inclusive accommodation at a 5* beach resort
- airport transfers

no single supplements

**Stopover in Dubai
2 nights £149 pp**

4

- ⊙ return   ○ one way

from

to

departure date
day   month

return date
day   month

passengers
1   adult
0   child
0   infant

5

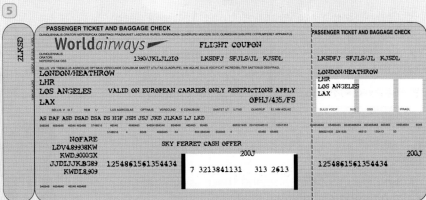

PASSENGER TICKET AND BAGGAGE CHECK

Worldairways   FLIGHT COUPON

LONDON/HEATHROW
LHR
LOS ANGELES   VALID ON EUROPEAN CARRIER ONLY RESTRICTIONS APPLY
LAX

NOFARE

SKY FERRET CASH OFFER

PASSENGER TICKET AND BAGGAGE CHECK

LONDON/HEATHROW
LHR
LOS ANGELES
LAX

6

7

Tourist destination regions (2006)

Country	Total visitors (million)	% change 06/05
1. France	79.1	4.2
2. Spain	58.5	4.5
3. USA	51.1	3.8
4. China	49.6	6.0
5. Italy	41.1	12.4
6. UK	30.7	9.3
7. Germany	23.6	9.6
8. Mexico	21.4	-2.6
9. Austria	20.3	1.5
10. Russian Federation	20.2	1.5

Source: World Tourism Organization

A You are a student in the School of Tourism and Hospitality Management of Hadford University.

    1 The title of your first lecture is *What is tourism?* Write a definition of tourism.

    2 What other ideas will be in this lecture? Make some notes.

    See *Skills bank*

B 🎧 Listen to Part 1 of the lecture.

    1 What is the lecturer going to talk about? Make a list.

    2 The lecturer mentions some reasons for studying tourism. Make a list.

C In Part 2, the lecturer talks about the impacts of tourism.

    1 What are the main impacts of tourism? Make a list.

    2 🎧 Listen to Part 2 of the lecture. Tick any points on your list. Add any extra points.

D In Part 3, the lecturer talks about some aspects of tourism.

    1 Copy Table 1 into your notebook. You will need space for 12 aspects.

    2 🎧 Listen to Part 3 of the lecture. Take notes and complete Table 1 with five aspects of tourism.

    3 Add examples of each aspect from your own experience.

E In Part 4 of the talk, the lecturer describes two more aspects of tourism.

    1 🎧 Listen to Part 4 and add these aspects to your table. Add examples.

    2 What three branches of tourism are mentioned? (Clue: look at the pictures!)

F In the final part of the talk, the lecturer discusses five more aspects of tourism.

    🎧 Listen to Part 5 and add these aspects to your table. Add examples.

G Rewrite your definition of tourism from Exercise A. Use words and ideas from Table 1.

H Look back at your notes from Exercise A. Did you predict:

    • the main ideas?

    • most of the special vocabulary?

Table 1:
Aspects of tourism (according to Leiper)

	Aspect	**Example**
1		
2		
3		
4		
5		

1.3 Extending skills

choosing the right kind of notes

A In tourism, what can you …

1 satisfy?	**4** book?	**7** foster?
2 change?	**5** pollute?	**8** engage in?
3 spend?	**6** embark on?	**9** tolerate?

B How can you organize information in a lecture? Match the beginnings and endings.

1 question and		contrast
2 problem and		definition
3 classification and		disadvantages
4 advantages and		effect
5 comparison and		events
6 cause and		supporting information
7 sequence of		process
8 stages of a		solution
9 theories or opinions then		answer

C How can you record information during a lecture? Match the illustrations with the words and phrases in the box.

> tree diagram   flowchart   headings and notes   spidergram   table   timeline   two columns

D Match each organization of information in Exercise B with a method of note-taking from Exercise C. You can use one method for different types of organization.

E 🎧 Listen to six lecture introductions. Choose a possible way to take notes from Exercise C in each case.

Example:

You hear: *I would like to define tourism as travel for the purpose of recreation, and the provision of services for this.*

You choose: *tree diagram* or *spidergram*

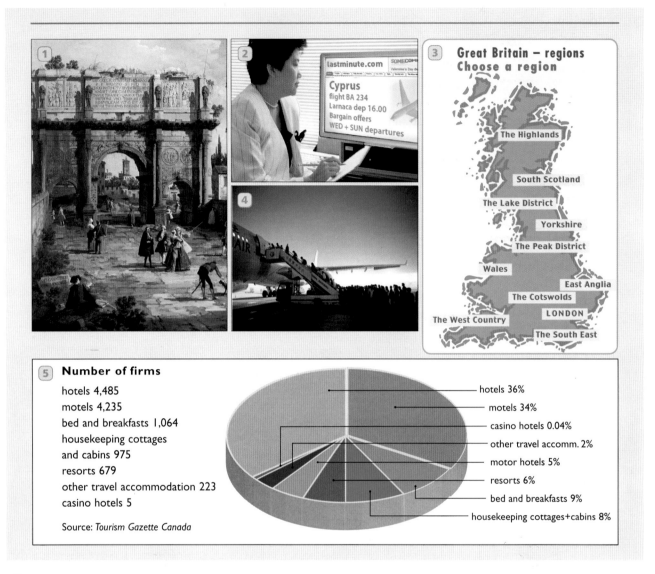

A Describe pictures 1–5 above. Use words from the box.

> hospitality   Grand Tour   mass travel   information   reservation   transport

B 🎧 Cover the opposite page. Listen to the lecture introductions from Lesson 3 again. Make an outline on a separate sheet of paper for each introduction.

C Look at your outline for each lecture. What do you expect the lecturer to talk about in the rest of the lecture? In what order?

D 🎧 Listen to the next part of each lecture. Complete your notes.

E Uncover the opposite page. Check your notes with the model notes. Are yours the same or different?

F Work in pairs.

   1 Use the notes on the opposite page. Reconstruct one lecture.

   2 Give the lecture to another pair.

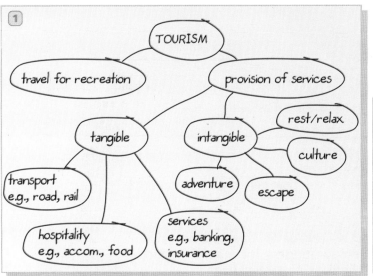

1

TOURISM
- travel for recreation
- provision of services
  - tangible
    - transport e.g., road, rail
    - hospitality e.g., accom., food
  - intangible
    - adventure
    - escape
    - services e.g., banking, insurance
  - rest/relax
  - culture

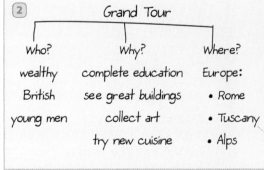

2 Grand Tour

Who?	Why?	Where?
wealthy	complete education	Europe:
British	see great buildings	• Rome
young men	collect art	• Tuscany
	try new cuisine	• Alps

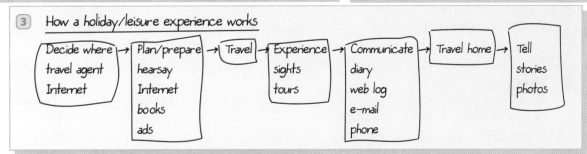

3 How a holiday/leisure experience works

Decide where (travel agent, Internet) → Plan/prepare (hearsay, Internet, books, ads) → Travel → Experience (sights, tours) → Communicate (diary, web log, e-mail, phone) → Travel home → Tell (stories, photos)

4

MASS TRAVEL
1 Two important factors
   1.1 Improvements in technology
   1.2 More leisure time

2 First examples
   2.1 Thomas Cook – first package tour

3 Target groups
   3.1 Victorians – upper + middle classes
   3.2 C20th – most people in dev. countries

5 UK TOURIST MARKET

Value tourism/hosp. industry	£74 bn
GDP	4.5%
Employees	2.1 m
Overseas tourists spend	£11 bn
Domestic spend	£59 bn
Tourism earnings league	7
Top five overseas markets	USA, France, Germany, Irish Rep., Netherlands
UK residents:	
vacations of one night or more	101 m
overnight business trips	23 m
overnight trips to friends and relatives	37 m

6 SPACE TOURISM – key developments

Date	Event
1950s	interest in rocket designs, space stations, moon bases
1985	passenger spacecraft designed: Phoenix
1989	space hotel design
1993	first market research survey on space tourism
1998	'X Prize' launched
2001	Dennis Tito – first paying space tourist
2004	Richard Branson plans hotel in space and regular space travel
2007	NASA and Branson's Virgin Galactic agree to collaborate in future manned space flight technology
2008	first space terminal built in New Mexico

Guessing words in context

Using related words

Sometimes a word in general English has a special meaning in tourism.

Examples:
package, book, promotion

If you recognize a word but don't understand it in context, think:
What is the basic meaning of the word? Does that help me understand the special meaning?

Example:
*A **package** is something you wrap up. A **package holiday** must mean a holiday which is wrapped up in some way. (It does – it is a holiday which has flights and accommodation and perhaps car hire all in one.)*

Removing prefixes

A **prefix** = letters at the **start of a word**.
A prefix changes the meaning of a word.

Examples:
reconfirm – confirm again
dissatisfaction – opposite of satisfaction

If you don't recognize a word, think:
Is there is a prefix? Remove it. Do you recognize the word now?
What does that prefix mean? Add it to the meaning of the word.

Removing suffixes

A **suffix** = letters at the **end of a word**.
A suffix sometimes changes the **part of speech** of the word.

Examples:
accommodate ➜ *accommodation* = verb ➜ noun
promotion ➜ *promotional* = noun ➜ adjective

A suffix sometimes changes the meaning **in a predictable way**.

Examples:
summar(y) + ize – make or make into
broad + en – make or make more
stress + ful – full of

If you don't recognize a word, think:
Is there a suffix? Remove it. Do you recognize the word now?
What does that suffix mean? Add it to the meaning of the word.

Making the most of lectures

Before a lecture ...

Plan
- Find out the topic of the lecture.
- Research the topic.
- Check the pronunciation of names and key words in English.

Prepare
- Get to the lecture room early.
- Sit where you can see and hear clearly.
- Bring any equipment you may need.
- Write the date, topic and name of the lecturer at the top of a sheet of paper.

During a lecture ...

Predict
- Listen carefully to the introduction. Think: *What kind of lecture is this?*
- Write an outline. Leave space for notes.
- Think of possible answers/solutions/effects, etc., while the lecturer is speaking.

Produce
- Write notes/copy from the board.
- Don't try to copy everything – you need time to look, listen, process what the lecturer is saying and write at the same time.
- Record sources – books/websites/names.
- At the end, ask the lecturer/other students for missing information.

Making perfect lecture notes

Choose the best way to record information from a lecture.

advantages and disadvantages	➜ two-column table
cause and effect	➜ spidergram
classification and definition	➜ tree diagram/spidergram
comparison and contrast	➜ table
facts and figures	➜ table
sequence of events	➜ timeline
stages of a process	➜ flowchart
question and answer	➜ headings and notes

Speaking from notes

Sometimes you have to give a short talk in a seminar on research you have done.
- Prepare the listeners with an introduction.
- Match the introduction to the type of information/notes.

2 WHAT'S YOUR KIND OF TOURISM?

2.1 Vocabulary — using an English–English dictionary

A How can an English–English dictionary help you understand and produce spoken and written English?

B Study the dictionary extract on the opposite page.
1 Why are the two words (top left and top right) important?
2 What do the words *tour*, *transport* and *trip* have in common?
3 How many meanings does *tour* (noun) have?
4 Are *transport* (noun) and *transport* (verb) pronounced exactly the same?
5 What adjective can you make from the word *tourist*?
6 How many ways can you pronounce the word *tourist*?
7 Where is the stress on *tourist trap*? How do you know?
8 Can you say *tourist classes*? Explain your answer.
9 What can you say about the spelling of the word *traveller*?
10 Can you say *We tripped to Dubai*. Explain your answer.

C Look at the bold words in the dictionary extract.
1 What order are they in?
2 Write the words in the blue box in the same order.

> accommodation   transport   lobby
> resort   luxury   experience
> independent   adventurous   budget
> development   itinerary   environment

D Look at the top of a double page from an English–English dictionary.
1 Which word from Exercise C will appear on these pages?
2 Think of words before and after some of the other words in Exercise C.

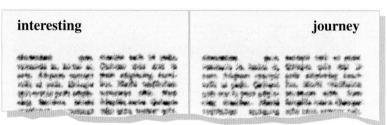

interesting   journey

E Look up the red words from the blue box in a dictionary.
1 How many meanings can you find for each word?
2 What kind of noun/verb is each word?
3 Which meaning is most likely in a tourism and hospitality text?

F Look up the green words.
1 Where is the stress in each word?
2 What is the sound of the underlined letter(s) in each word?
3 Use each of these words in a sentence about tourism or hospitality.

G Test each other on the words from Exercises E and F. Give the dictionary definition of one of the words. Can your partner guess which word you are defining?

H What do the pictures on the opposite page show? Use some of the words from this lesson.

tour

tour /tʊə(r)/ n 1. [C] a journey during which you visit several places of interest: *a tour around the British Isles* 2. a short trip through or to a place in order to see it: *They took a guided tour of the palace.*

tour v [I, T] to visit as a tourist: *I'll be touring around Canada this year.*

tourism /'tʊərɪzəm/ n [U] 1. the practice of travelling for pleasure, esp. on holiday 2. the business of providing holiday services, tours, hotels, etc. for tourists

tourist /'tʊərɪst/ /'tɔːrɪst/ n a person travelling for pleasure

touristy /'tʊərɪsti/ adj full of tourists: *The seaside towns are very touristy now.*

tourist class /'tʊərɪst klɑːs/ [U] travelling prices and conditions on planes, trains, etc. suitable for travellers who do not wish to spend much money

'tourist office n [C] an office that provides information for people who are visiting an area or town

'tourist trap n [C] a crowded place which provides entertainment or things to buy for tourists, often at high prices

tripper

transport /'trænspɔːt/ AmE **transportation** n [U] a system of vehicles, such as buses, trains, planes, etc. for getting from one place to another: *The Tokyo transport system is very efficient.*

transport /træn'spɔːt/ v [T] to carry goods or people from one place to another

travel v /'trævl/ [I, T] 1. to make a journey from one place to another: *They travelled to Hong Kong.* 2. [I] to move from one place to another: *Light travels faster than sound.*

traveller /'trævələ(r)/ AmE **traveler** n [C] someone who travels

trip /trɪp/ n [C] a short visit for business or pleasure

trip v 1. [I] to lose your balance after walking into something: *I tripped on a step.* 2. [T] (trip up) to make someone fall by putting your foot in front of them

tripper /'trɪpə(r)/ n [C] someone who visits a place briefly, often with a large group of other people: *Many day trippers go to the seaside.*

A How many kinds of tourism can you think of?

B Study the text from *Tourism Today*.

 1 Define each type of tourism.

 2 Find a picture of each type.

C Discuss these questions.

 1 Have you experienced any of the types of tourism on this page?

 2 Which is/would be your favourite type of tourism? Why?

D You are going to read a text. What should you do before you read a text in detail?
See *Skills bank*

E This text is about a special type of tourism.

 1 Read the heading. What kind of tourism do you think this text is about?

 2 Think of three research questions before you read.

F Study these topic sentences from the text.

 1 What will the paragraphs describe?

 2 Which paragraphs are likely to answer your research questions?

> Many students go backpacking in their gap year, that once-in-a-lifetime period between school and college, or college and work.

> Backpacking is a great way to travel, they say.

> Backpackers are proud that they 'rough it'.

> Flashpacking is the latest development in personal tourism.

> Flashpackers are looking for adventure like backpackers, but there is one important difference.

> Travel companies are cashing in on this development.

> There are three countries where flashpacking works particularly well.

> First, there's Australia.

> Thailand is very cheap, relatively speaking.

> Finally, Argentina is enjoying a boom from three types of traveller.

G Read the full article now and check your ideas.

Tourism Today
Tourism in the 21st century

Do you think tourists only go to the beach? In this month's magazine, we look at all of these ... **and more!**

- Adventure tourism
- Agritourism
- Backpacking
- Cultural tourism
- Disaster tourism
- Ecotourism
- Events tourism
- Educational tourism
- Heritage tourism
- Health tourism
- Sports tourism
- Space tourism

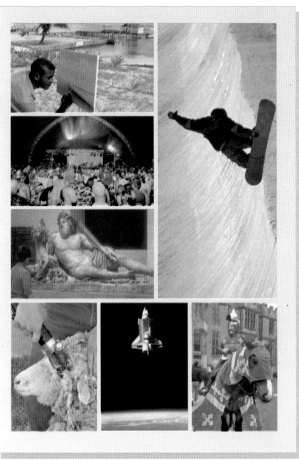

Backpacking …

or flashpacking?

Many students go backpacking in their gap year, that once-in-a-lifetime period between school and college, or college and work. Have you considered going to a foreign country thousands of miles away, all on your own? Could you cope without plane tickets, car-hire vouchers and booked accommodation?

Backpacking is a great way to travel, they say. As a backpacker, you're free to do what you want, within your shoestring budget, of course. You only need clothes, a passport and an independent spirit. You have no itinerary, except for some vague plans to 'do' Asia or 'go walking' in the Rockies. There's no tour operator to hold your hand.

Backpackers are proud that they 'rough it'. They are free and adventurous. But do they really have fun, hitching on dusty roads, sleeping in uncomfortable lodging houses, eating poor-quality food and wandering aimlessly through towns with no interest for the tourist? Perhaps they should wait until they can be a flashpacker.

Flashpacking is the latest development in personal tourism. As a flashpacker, you get the best of both worlds: the joy of real travel, but also luxury accommodation and transport when you want it.

Flashpackers are looking for adventure like backpackers, but there is one important difference. They have money. They are usually in their thirties and forties. They may be on extended holidays or career breaks. They probably went backpacking in their youth and think they are doing it all over again. But unlike your average gap-year student, they will spend what it takes to get the experience they are after. That outback tour of Central Australia costs £5000? Where's the 4WD? Start the engine!

Travel companies are cashing in on this development. They are selling round-the-world tickets like hot cakes. Greg Halpin, a 39-year-old marketing director, is a typical example: 'Flashpacking is a perfect word for what I've done. When I've changed jobs, I've used the break to go travelling. The last time, I went for six weeks, around Kenya and Tanzania. I put the trip together as I went along. I visited safari parks – some upmarket, some not. Then I went to Zanzibar, where I checked into a very flash hotel. It's always interesting doing that when you've been on the road. You turn up a bit grubby, with a dusty old backpack, and they look rather alarmed. They're very relieved an hour later, though, when you've cleaned up and walk back across the lobby looking decent. That's one essential tip for travelling this way: always keep a set of smart clothes in a plastic bag inside your pack.'

There are three countries where flashpacking works particularly well. Each one can offer some of the most enjoyable aspects of budget travel – adventure, cultural insights, earthy simplicity – but with plenty of choice along the way.

First, there's Australia. It's no surprise that Oz is well set up for budget travel, with a good network of cheap accommodation, silver beaches and the outback. Every Australian was a backpacker once. On the other hand, the Aussies have got a bit flash recently – cultural events, fancy cooking, etc. It adds up to perfect flashpacker territory.

Thailand is very cheap, relatively speaking. The temptation is to be all flash and no pack. After all, when an upmarket Bangkok restaurant only charges £10 per head, why settle for anything less? But you should. If you use your money to spoil yourself all the time, you'll never touch the real character and excitement of Thailand. So stay in that £4 beach hut, eat that 50p street snack and only buy yourself luxury when you really need it.

Finally, Argentina is enjoying a boom from three types of traveller. Gap-year kids have added the Andes to their list; holiday travellers are arriving in well-organized groups to trek around the countryside and now flashpackers have discovered that the continent has exactly their mix of wild adventures and home comforts. ■

2.3 Extending skills
topic sentences • summarizing

A Study the words in box a. They are all from the text in Lesson 2.

a flash spirit rough break smart boom

   1 Give two common meanings of each word.

   2 Choose the meaning of the word in the text.

   3 Check with your dictionary.

B Study the words in box b. They are all from the text in Lesson 2.

b independent adventurous uncomfortable development accommodation simplicity

   1 What is the base word in each case? What is the part of speech of the base word?

   2 Does the prefix/suffix change the part of speech?

   3 How does the prefix/suffix change the meaning of the base word?

C Look back at the topic sentences from the text in Lesson 2 (Exercise F, page 16). Don't look at the text on page 17. What information comes after each topic sentence? Suggest content.

   Example:

> Backpacking is a great way to travel, they say.

Advantages of backpacking, e.g., freedom, cheapness ...

D Write a summary of the text on page 17. Paraphrase the topic sentences. Add extra information and examples.

   See *Skills bank*

2.4 Extending skills
using research questions • writing topic sentences • summarizing

A Can you remember the different types of tourism from Lesson 2? List as many as you can remember and describe their meaning.

B You are going to read about a special type of tourism that is very popular.

   1 Give your definition of ecotourism. Then check with the first paragraph of the text on the opposite page.

   2 What conditions must Praia do Forte satisfy, according to TIES, to be an eco-resort?

   3 What is the best way to record information about the resort while you are reading?

C Study Alison Marshall's report.

   1 Highlight the topic sentences.

   2 Read each topic sentence. What will you find in the rest of the paragraph?

   3 Which paragraphs will probably tell you if Praia do Forte is an eco-resort? Read those paragraphs and make notes.

D Use the Internet to research one of the types of tourism described in Lesson 2.

   1 Write three research questions.

   2 Make notes.

   3 Write a series of topic sentences which summarize your findings.

   4 Report back to the other students. Read out each topic sentence then add extra details.

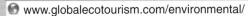

www.globalecotourism.com/environmental/

Ecotourism – is it as green as it is painted?

More and more travellers realize that tourism has an effect on the environment. Ecotourism is a result of this growing awareness. According to the International Ecotourism Society (TIES), ecotourism is 'responsible travel to natural areas that conserves the environment and improves the well-being of local people.' Ecotourists or organizers should make sure the impact on the environment is as small as possible. They should provide positive experiences for both visitors and hosts, and create financial benefits and a feeling of empowerment for local people.

Brazil is an example of a country which is developing ecotourism. Praia do Forte claims to be Brazil's first eco-resort. We sent our reporter, Alison Marshall, to check out its green credentials.

The environmental impact of travel is huge. Did you know that a return flight from London to Brazil releases 2,606 kg of carbon dioxide per passenger into the atmosphere? That's four times the annual carbon emissions of an average African. So just getting to the country damages the world environment. Then there's the long drive from the airport to the resort through the rainforest in a taxi on its last wheels. I'm beginning to wonder if this kind of tourism can be 'green' at all.

I try to be 'green' in my everyday life. I recycle the Sunday papers, and all my light bulbs are those expensive ones that last for ages, but I also really enjoy driving around London, and can never quite remember to turn the tap off when I'm brushing my teeth. Was this trip part of the green me or the other one?

Praia do Forte calls itself Brazil's first 'eco-resort'. The four-star, 247-bedroom hotel was opened by a Swiss–Brazilian industrialist who bought up 30,000 hectares

of subtropical rainforest to the north of Salvador. The resort's motto is 'use without abuse'. It says it can cater for tourists without damaging the environment.

The hotel certainly makes good use of the environment. There are forest hikes, river kayaking expeditions and moonlit walks to the silver beaches, where you can watch turtles lay their eggs. Biologists and guides accompany tourists on all these trips. They really try to show people the natural beauty of the area. They use local people as guides, and educate and train the local community.

There are some features I do not like as much. For example, they have built a village for employees next door to the resort. They use the village as a toy town which the hotel maps refer to as 'the fishermen's village'. It has been nicely done, and it is a lively and pleasant place. No doubt it brings financial benefits to the local economy but the little sandy strip is for the holidaymaker. There are no fishermen in sight.

However, perhaps it is unfair to criticize Praia do Forte for the things it could do better. It is a really lovely resort, and they are serious about the environment. Praia do Forte is not really green, in other words, but it is greener than many other resorts. If you are going to build something right in the middle of a natural paradise, then it is much better to build it like this. It is, after all, better to recycle the Sunday papers than to do nothing at all about the environment.

Using your English–English dictionary

This kind of dictionary helps you actually **learn** English.

Using headwords and parts of speech

1 Find the correct **headword**.

These **bold** words in a dictionary are in alphabetical order. Look at the words on the top left and top right of the double page. Find a word which comes just before and after your word.

2 Find the correct **meaning**.

If there are different meanings of the word, they appear in a numbered list. Look at all the meanings before you choose the correct one in context.

3 Find the correct **part of speech**.

Sometimes the same headword appears more than once, followed by a small number. This means the word has more than one part of speech, e.g., *n* and *v*. Work out the part of speech before you look up a word. Clues:

- Nouns come after articles (*a/an/the*) or adjectives.
- Verbs come after nouns or pronouns.

Learning to pronounce words

The symbols after the headword show you how to pronounce the word. Learn these symbols (the key is usually at the front or the back of the dictionary).

The little line in the symbols shows you how to stress the word.
Example:
tourist /ˈtʊərɪst/

Learning to use words correctly in context

Nouns can be **countable** or **uncountable**. This information is important for using articles and verb forms (e.g., *is/are*) correctly. Look for the symbol [C] or [U].

Some verbs need an object. They are **transitive**. Some verbs don't need an object. They are **intransitive**. This information is important for making good sentences. Look for the symbol [T] or [I].

Some words can be spelt in **British** English (e.g., *colour, traveller*) or **American** English (e.g., *color, traveler*). Choose the correct spelling for the text you are working on.

Skills bank

Doing reading research

Before you start reading ...

- Think of research questions. In other words, ask yourself: *What must I find out from my research?*
- Look at headings, sub-headings, illustrations. Look for patterns or variations in presentation, e.g., a series of dates; words in **bold** or *italic* script. Think: *What information do they give me?*
- Decide how to record information from your reading. Choose one or more methods of note-taking. **See Unit 1** *Skills bank*

While you are reading ...

- Highlight the topic sentences.
- Think: *Which paragraph(s) will probably give me the answer to my research questions?*
- Read these paragraph(s) first.
- Make notes.

After reading ...

- Think: *Did the text answer all my research questions?*

Using topic sentences to summarize

The topic sentences of a text normally make a good basis for a summary. Follow this procudure:

- Locate the topic sentences.
- Paraphrase them – in other words, rewrite them in your own words so that the meaning is the same. Do not simply copy them. (This is a form of plagiarism.)
- Add supporting information – once again, in your own words.

Example:

Paraphrase of topic sentence	*Tourists are becoming aware of what their travel does to the environment.*
Supporting information and examples (summarized)	*There is a growing number of green resorts.*

- Check your summary. Check that the ideas flow logically. Check spelling and grammar. If your summary is short, it may be just one paragraph. Divide a longer summary into paragraphs.

3 HOSPITALITY RESEARCH

3.1 Vocabulary   stress within words

A Study the two sentences on the right.

> *My parents were famous for their hospitality. People loved coming to stay for the weekend.*

> *He works for a hospitality company. They get tickets for all the top theatre shows and sporting events in London.*

1 What is the key difference in the meaning of *hospitality* in the two sentences?

2 What is the relationship between the two meanings?

B Study Figure 1 on the opposite page.

1 What process is shown here?

2 Copy and complete the notes on the right with words from the diagram.

3 🎧 Listen and check your ideas.

4 Where is the main stress in each multi-syllable word in Figure 1?

> *A restaurant purchases food, which it . . ., . . . and . . . to customers who . . .*
>
> *The prices reflect the investment in . . ., . . ., . . .*

C Use a word from Figure 1 or the texts above to complete each of these sentences. Change the form if necessary.

1 The _____ in the restaurant's kitchen is very modern, which makes food preparation easy.

2 One cannot run any business without the right _____ .

3 Countries hosting sporting _____ like the World Cup need to make sure they have enough hotel accommodation.

4 Good _____ is essential in the hospitality industry.

5 Before you open a new restaurant, you must _____ your market carefully.

6 A restaurant needs to _____ good food and give value for money.

D Study the words in the blue box.

1 What is the relationship between all the words?

2 Can you see four logical groups?

3 Check your ideas with Figure 2 on the opposite page.

4 Where is the main stress in each multi-syllable word?

> aeroplane   airport   bar
> casino   cinema   hospital
> office   prison   restaurant
> school   theme park   train

E Match the words to make phrases related to hospitality.

1	hospitality	association
2	real	behaviour
3	kitchen	systems
4	food	equipment
5	information	estate
6	consumer	industry
7	quantitative	methods
8	industry	science

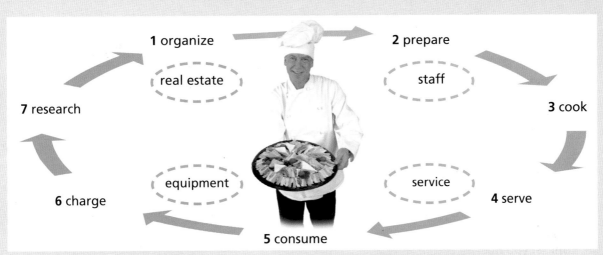

Figure 1: *Hospitality in the restaurant trade*

Freestanding businesses

hotels

holiday centres

cruise ships

time-share

bars

restaurants

Leisure venues

casinos

night clubs

cinemas

theatres

sports stadia

theme parks

health clubs

attractions

Travel venues

airports

train stations

bus stations

ferry terminals

aeroplanes

trains

ferries

Subsidized hospitality

workplaces

hospitals

education

military

prisons

retailers

Figure 2: *Hospitality outlets*

A Study the slide on the right and the handout from a lecture at the bottom of this page.

    1 What do you expect to hear in this lecture? Make a list.

    2 Write down some key words you expect to hear.

    3 Check the pronunciation of the key words with other students or with a dictionary.

    4 How are you going to prepare for this lecture?

B 🎧 Listen to Part 1 of the lecture.

    1 What exactly is the lecturer going to talk about? Look at the list of topics on the right. Tick the topic(s) you heard.

    2 Why is the lecturer talking about hospitality research?

    3 What is a good way to organize notes for this lecture?

C 🎧 Listen to Part 2 of the lecture.

    1 What is the main purpose of this section?

    2 What two kinds of hospitality does the lecturer identify?

D 🎧 Listen to Part 3 of the lecture.

    1 What is the meaning of the word *approach* in hospitality research?

    2 What is the *environment* which the lecturer mentions?

    3 What examples does the lecturer give to help you understand the following aspects of the management approach?

- the external environment
- human resources
- the technical infrastructure
- management information systems

    4 What do you expect to hear in the next part of the lecture?

E 🎧 Listen to Part 4 of the lecture.

    1 What purposes do Taylor and Edgar see for hospitality research?

    2 What makes research

- positivist or scientific?
- normative?

F Study the *Skills bank*. Use phrases to check your understanding of information in this lecture. Complete the table in the handout on the right.

Topics

computer systems _____

hospitality _____

legislation _____

personnel _____

research history _____

research methods _____

research theories _____

researchers _____

the restaurant industry _____

tourism _____

🍁 **HADFORD** *University*

Faculty: Tourism and Hospitality

Hospitality research

1990s	Littlejohn	scientific approach
		_____ approach
Late 90s	Taylor & _____	discovery management _____
_____	Lashley & Morrison	social domain _____ domain _____ domain

3.3 Extending skills

stress within words • using information sources • reporting findings

A 🎧 Listen to some stressed syllables. Identify the word below in each case. Number each word.

Example:

You hear: *1 da* /deɪ/ You write:

accommodate	____	consume	____	industry	____
accommodation	*1*	entertainment	____	investment	____
association	____	equipment	____	purchase	____
casino	____	facilities	____	subsidized	____

B Where is the main stress in each multi-syllable word in Exercise A?

1 Mark the main stress.

2 Practise saying each word.

C Work in pairs or groups. Define one of the words in Exercise A. The other student(s) must find and say the correct word.

D Pronounce these words related to doing research.

1 Mark the stress on each word.

2 Write an example sentence with each word.

> academic   approach   argue   behaviour   consider   contribute   define   journal
> normative   performance   practitioner   qualitative   quantitative   reflect   review

E Before you attend a lecture you should do some research.

1 How could you research the lecture topics on the right?

2 What information should you record?

3 How could you record the information?

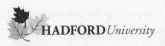

HADFORD *University*

Faculty: Tourism and Hospitality

1   Hospitality and tourism

2   Systems theory in hospitality research

3   Hospitality education

F You are going to do some research on a particular lecture topic. You must find:

1 a dictionary definition

2 an encyclopedia explanation

3 a useful Internet site

> **Student A**
> • Do some research on **hospitality**.
> • Tell your partner about your findings.

> **Student B**
> • Do some research on **hospitality systems theory**.
> • Tell your partner about your findings.

A You are going to listen to a continuation of the lecture in Lesson 2.

    1 Make a list of points from that lecture.

    2 What is the lecturer going to talk about now?

    3 🎧 Listen to Part 4 of the lecture again and check your ideas.

B Look at the handout on the opposite page.

    1 What do you think are the key ideas of the hospitality science and hospitality management approaches? The illustrations on the handout may help you.

    2 🎧 Listen to Part 5 of the lecture and check your ideas.

    3 What is a good way to make notes? Prepare a page in your notebook.

C 🎧 Listen to Part 6 of the lecture. Make notes. Ask other students for information.

D 🎧 Listen to Part 7 of the lecture. What is the main difference between the hospitality systems theory and the other approaches?

E 🎧 Listen to Parts 5–7 of the lecture again and say whether these sentences are true (T) or false (F).

    1 The approaches the lecturer discusses do not overlap. _____

    2 Researchers following the hospitality science approach publish a lot in tourism journals. _____

    3 The hospitality management school is mainly interested in facts. _____

    4 The hospitality studies school is based mainly in America. _____

    5 Lashley and Morrison are representatives of the school that focuses on experiences and relationships. _____

    6 The systems theory approach doesn't look at one specific aspect of hospitality. _____

    7 Neil Leiper is a representative of the hospitality management school. _____

F Imagine you had to report this lecture to a student who was absent.

    1 Study the transcript on pages 115–117. Find and underline or highlight key sections of the lecture.

    2 Find and underline key sentences from the lecture.

    3 Make sure you can say the sentences with good pronunciation.

    4 Compare your ideas in groups.

G Describe a possible research project for each of these theories in the hospitality industry. What could researchers decide to research?

- hospitality science
- hospitality management
- hospitality studies
- hospitality experiences
- hospitality systems

HADFORD *University*

Faculty: Tourism and Hospitality

Hospitality research

These notes go with the hospitality research lecture.
The images might give you a hint as to the kind of research in this area.

Hospitality science

The first approach focuses on what people eat and
do when they are enjoying hospitality.

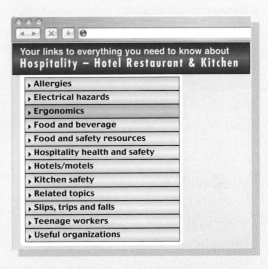

Your links to everything you need to know about
Hospitality – Hotel Restaurant & Kitchen

- Allergies
- Electrical hazards
- Ergonomics
- Food and beverage
- Food and safety resources
- Hospitality health and safety
- Hotels/motels
- Kitchen safety
- Related topics
- Slips, trips and falls
- Teenage workers
- Useful organizations

Hospitality management

The second approach looks at collecting data
about consumer behaviour and preferences to
improve services. This approach often has a
marketing dimension.

ABX Marketing Solutions   **Tel 8876543**   **info@abx.com**

- about us
- request info
- photo gallery
- recent projects
- contact us
- OUR PORTFOLIO
- photography
- creative design
- hospitality marketing solutions

The Stella Group wanted their cruise ships
photographed for their website and promotional
materials.
Click here for more information.

Never underestimate your looks ... Both you and your
product always need to look the best they can.
A visual image is much more powerful than the written
word. Images make customers remember you and
motivate them to do business with you.
At **ABX Marketing Solutions**, we offer you a unique

package of design, photography and hospitality
marketing. All these work together to get your message
across in ways your customers can't ignore.
ABX has been around for years. Our portfolio is so
diverse that we can tackle any industry – we are able to
understand your business!

Hospitality studies

The third approach deals with . . .

Stress within words

Nouns, verbs, adjectives and adverbs are called content words because they carry the meaning.

One-syllable words

Some content words have one syllable or sound. This is always stressed.

Examples: 'host, 'chef, 'staff

Two-syllable words

Some content words have two syllables. Two-syllable nouns and adjectives are often stressed on the first syllable. Two-syllable verbs are often stressed on the second syllable.

Examples:

Nouns	'outlet, 'venue
Adjectives	'dirty, 'tranquil
Verbs	pre'pare, con'sume

Exceptions:

Nouns	de'bate, do'main, de'sign
Adjectives	u'nique, se'rene
Verbs	'travel, 'purchase

Multi-syllable words

Some content words have three or more syllables. Multi-syllable words are often stressed three syllables from the end.

Example:

Ooo   oOoo   ooOoo

This is true for most words ending in:

~ise/ ~ize	'advertise, 'organize
~sis	a'nalysis, hy'pothesis
~ate	a'ccommodate
~ify	'classify, 'specify
~ical	techno'logical
~able	hos'pitable
~ular	par'ticular, 'regular
~ive	'normative

Exceptions:

Multi-syllable words ending in the following letters are normally stressed two syllables from the end.

~ance	per'formance
~ic	aca'demic
~tion	att'raction
~sion	dis'cussion
~ent	e'quipment
~al	ex'ternal

Getting information from other people

From the lecturer

We can sometimes ask a lecturer questions at the end of a lecture. Introduce each question in a polite or tentative way.

Examples:
Could you go over the bit about systems theory *again*?
I didn't quite understand what you said about the hospitality industry.
I wonder if you could repeat the name of the researchers who reviewed the debate?
Would you mind giving the source of that quotation *again*?

From other students

It is a good idea to ask other students after a lecture for information to complete your notes.

Examples:
What did the lecturer say about management information systems?
Why did he tell that story about the restaurant?
I didn't get the bit about the technical infrastructure.

Be polite!

It sometimes sounds impolite to ask people a direct question. We often add a polite introduction.

Examples:
Has food science anything to do with hospitality?
➜ *Do you know if* food science has anything to do with hospitality?

What does 'normative' mean?
➜ *Can you remember what* 'normative' means?

Reporting information to other people

We often have to report research findings to a tutor or other students in a seminar. Make sure you can give:
- sources – books, articles, writers, publication dates
- quotes – in the writer's own words
- summary findings – in your own words

4 CAREERS IN TOURISM AND HOSPITALITY

A Study the words in box a.

1 Which words or phrases relate to computers and the Internet? Which relate to books and libraries? Find two groups of words.

2 Find pairs of words and phrases with similar meanings, one from each group.

3 Check your ideas with the *Research words* box on the opposite page.

a
books   browse/search   catalogue
close   cross-reference   database
electronic resources   exit/log off
hyperlink   index   library   log in/log on
look up   menu   open   page
search engine results   table of contents
web page   World Wide Web

B Complete the instructions for using the Learning Resource Centre with words or phrases from box a.

C Study the abbreviations in box b and box c.

1 What do the abbreviations in box b refer to?

2 What do the abbreviations in box c refer to?

3 What does each abbreviation mean?

4 Read *Career update* and *Tourism abbreviations* on the opposite page. Check your ideas.

5 How do you say each of the abbreviations?

D Study the acronyms in box d.

1 What do all these acronyms refer to?

2 What does each acronym mean?

3 Check the meanings on the Internet.

4 How do you say each of the acronyms?

See *Vocabulary bank*

E Study the nouns in box e.

1 Make a verb from each noun.

2 Make another noun from the verb.

HADFORD *University*

Learning Resource Centre

Instructions for use:

You need to find out about careers in tourism, hospitality and leisure. If you want to access web pages on the _____ , you must first _____ to the university Intranet with your username and password. You can use any _____ but the default is Google. _____ for web pages by typing one or more keywords in the search box and clicking on **Search**, or pressing **Enter**. When the results appear, click on a _____ (highlighted in blue) to go to the web page. Click on **Back** to return to the results listing. You can also use the university _____ of learning resources. Click on **Careers in Tourism** on the main _____ .

b
CEO   CFO   COO   DOO   GM
HRD   MD

c
AIT   APD   ARR   B&B   BABA   F&B
FIT   IT   QA   T&T   TIC   TIP   VAT

d
ACE   ANTOR   BATO   ETOUR
NAITA   VISTA

e
class   computer   digit
identity   machine

Career update

Who's who in the T&T business,
and could this be you?

Jennifer Saunders has taken on the role of general manager sales at Amco hotels. She will oversee sales activities in Thailand. She was recently director of sales at Brink's Inc.

Lauren Ko has moved into the position of chief executive officer of China Trade International. Ko has been involved in the operational side for many years.

Leon Gonzales has been appointed regional HR director for the Brazil Eco Resorts chain. He has been transferred from the position of marketing manager.

Imran Hussain has been promoted to managing director of Skydiving Inc., an international group of leisure events companies.

John Summers has been named chief operations officer at the British Tourist Authority in the UK. Summers was working as director of operations for the Coca-Cola Company.

Sarah Brinkman joins the rooms division of the Ritz-Carlton as chief financial officer. She was previously director of housekeeping at the Ritz in Los Angeles.

Claudio Ruegger has moved to the new role of reservations manager at the Grand Hyatt Muscat. Prior to this position he was events supervisor for the SKYCITY in Auckland.

Research words

Are you doing research on the web? Many web research words have common equivalents.

Research word or phrase	Common word or phrase for printed information
electronic resources	books
search engine results	index
hyperlink	cross-reference
database	catalogue
World Wide Web	library
menu	table of contents
browse/search	look up
web page	page
log in/log on	open
exit/log off	close

Tourism abbreviations

AIT	air inclusive tour
APD	air passenger duty
ARR	average room rate
B&B	bed and breakfast
BABA	book-a-bed-ahead
F&B	food and beverage
(F)IT	(fully) inclusive tour
QA	quality assurance
T&T	tourism and travel
TIC/P	tourist information centre/point
VAT	value added tax

A Discuss these questions.

1 What careers do you associate with the tourism, hospitality and leisure industry?

2 There are more jobs in this industry now than twenty years ago. What development in society has caused this?

3 How can you succeed in this industry?

B Look at the title of the text on the opposite page.

1 What exactly does it mean?

2 What would you like to know about this topic? Make a list of questions.

C One student wrote down ideas about careers before reading the text on the opposite page.

1 Write **A** (I agree), **D** (I disagree) or **?** (I'm not sure) next to the ideas on the right.

2 Add any other ideas you have.

D Read all the topic sentences.

1 What is the structure of this text? Choose Structure A or B (below right).

2 What do you expect to find in each paragraph?

E Read the text and check your predictions.

F Discuss these questions.

1 People perceive the industry in a certain way. What is the effect of that perception?

2 What characteristics does employment in this industry generally have?

3 Which ways into a career are described in the article?

G Topics sometimes develop inside a paragraph.

1 Does the topic develop in each paragraph of the text? If so, underline the word or words which introduce the change.

2 What is the effect of the word or words on the development of the topic?

See Skills bank

People's view of the tourism industry is usually incorrect. ___

There is a wide range of possible careers in tourism. ___

Hospitality is something that has only limited effects on our lives. ___

It's hard to use tourism skills in other areas of society. ___

There are about 125,000 tourism businesses worldwide. ___

The key skill in tourism is dealing with people. ___

The tourism industry makes high demands on flexibility of its staff. ___

The best way to get into tourism is through a traineeship. ___

Qualifications are valuable but personality is more important. ___

Structure A

Para	Contents
1	People's perceptions of the industry
2	The nature of employment in the industry
3	What kind of people are suited to the industry
4	How to get a job in the industry

Structure B

Para	Contents
1	Jobs in the tourism, leisure and hospitality industry
2	Other employment sectors
3	Desirable personality traits to work in the industry
4	How to qualify to work in the industry

Careering uphill: opportunities for employment in the TTH sector

Most people, when they consider a career in tourism, hospitality or leisure, think of waiters and chefs, fitness instructors and travel agents. Obviously, these people don't really know the tourism industry very well. They see an industry that offers part-time, low-paid jobs in hotels or restaurants, jobs that people do until they find a 'real' career. Needless to say, that type of career is part of tourism, but there is so much more. Interior designers, marketing agents, event planners, museum curators and hiking guides are all part of the industry, too. In the same way, hospitality is not just about hotels. It affects us every day. We grab a sandwich for lunch, stop off for a coffee or drinks with friends, stay at a hotel, go to the cinema or theatre, eat in a canteen at work, catch a train, get fuel at a motorway service station. All this falls within the scope of hospitality.

World T&T economy employment was estimated at 234,305,000 jobs in 2006, 8.7% of total employment, or 1 in every 11.5 jobs. By 2016, this should total 279,347,000 jobs, 9% of total employment or one in every 11.1 jobs. (WTTC, 2006)

Tourism-related employment is different from many other employment sectors. For one thing, tourism is a highly mobile industry. Also, the skills learnt in most tourism occupations are easily transferable to other sectors in the industry. What you learn in, say, accommodation, you can apply to transportation, F&B services, event and conference planning, attractions, tourism services, outdoor adventure and recreation. Fortunately, these skills transfer to just about anywhere in the world, which makes it one of the most flexible industries. If you are really dedicated, the industry also enables you to rise quickly on the career ladder. Moreover, there are a large number of people who take advantage of the flexibility offered by the tourism industry to work on a part-time basis. Finally, statistics do not always show the benefits offered to many tourism employees, such as clothing and footwear allowances, dry cleaning services, free meals, and staff discounts (such as cheap flights).

This makes working in the TTH sector sound appealing, but it may not be suitable for everybody. Certainly, it's an industry that is constantly expanding and opening up opportunities for interesting careers. It sounds great, doesn't it? Travel, see the world, meet people: but that's not really what the industry is about. Like any job or career, it's what you make it, and of course the variety of this sector is enormous: 125,000 tourism businesses exist in the UK alone and 1.75 million people are employed in these businesses. So what sort of person do you need to be to work in hospitality, leisure and tourism? It's not an open door. You need to like people, and to enjoy the challenge of working in an environment focused on the customer. This means putting up with customers' dissatisfaction. You need to be flexible, adaptable, to enjoy problem-solving, and to be able to think on your feet. It goes without saying that you need to be able to work as part of a team.

World T&T generated US$6,477.2 bn of economic activity in 2006. This is expected to grow to US$12,118.6 bn by 2016. (WTTC, 2006)

Not surprisingly, in such a varied world, there are many ways of entering the industry. So, what's the best way, and what qualifications do you need? You can simply get a job and benefit from company training and development, possibly alongside a part-time course. Many hotels and restaurants also offer apprentice or traineeship schemes, which combine training in the workplace with time to study. Alternatively, you can enrol in a full-time college or university course. Qualifications alone, however, are no guarantee of a job. Much depends on your personality, attitude, communication skills and common sense. The variety of responsibilities, the chance to work with people from around the world, the potential for quick growth, training opportunities and benefits: these are just some of the many reasons that attract hundreds of thousands of tourism employees across the world and keep them interested in this dynamic industry.

A Discuss these questions.

1 You want to find out about careers in tourism, hospitality and leisure. Where would you look for the information? Why?

2 What keywords would you use to make this search? Why?

B Your search produces 50 results. How can you select the most useful ones without reading all of them? Look at the list of criteria on the right and put a tick or '?'.

C You have some more research tasks (below). Choose up to four keywords or phrases for each search.

1 Which country employs most people in the tourism industry?

2 How many people are employed in the UK hospitality industry?

3 What human resource careers are there in the tourism sector?

D Go to a computer and try out your chosen keywords.

> Criteria for choosing to read a result
>
> It contains all of my keywords. ____
> The document comes from a journal. ____
> It is in the first ten results. ____
> It has this year's date. ____
> It is a large document. ____
> The website address ends in .org ____
> The website address ends in .edu ____
> The website address contains .ac ____
> It is a PDF file. ____
> It refers to tourism. ____
> It refers to a person I know (of). ____
> It refers to an organization I know (of).
>
> ____

A What information is contained in the results listing of a search engine?

1 Make a list.

2 Check with the results listings on the opposite page.

B Scan the results listings. Answer these questions.

1 What keywords were entered?

2 Why was *journal* used as a keyword?

C Answer these questions.

1 Which results contain abbreviations or acronyms?

2 Where is each website address?

3 Where is the size of each document?

4 Are there any PDF documents?

5 Do any results give dates?

6 Why are the words in different colours?

7 Which result has all the keywords?

8 Which results refer to journals?

9 Which results come from educational sites?

10 Which results come from commercial sites?

11 What does *similar pages* mean?

12 What does *cached* mean?

D Continue your research on careers in the tourism, hospitality and leisure industry now by entering the keywords into a search engine and accessing three of the results. Compare your findings with other students.

E Choose the most interesting result. Write a paragraph about the information you discovered. Develop the topic within the paragraph with discourse markers and stance markers.

Web | Images | Groups | News | Froogle | Maps | more »

[Search] Advanced Search
Preferences

Web   Results **1 - 10** of about **316,000** for...**(0.42 seconds)**

(1) Altis: The Guide to Internet Resources in **Hospitality**, **Leisure** ...
Hospitality, **Leisure**, Sport and **Tourism** Adding Value and Employability is a joint ... and separate sections for **employers** and **recruiters**, containing FAQs, ...
altis.ac.uk/browse/127/278.page1.html - 22k - Cached - Similar pages

(2) Altis: The Guide to Internet Resources in **Hospitality**, **Leisure** ...
... and the **Journal** of **Hospitality**, **Leisure**, Sport and **Tourism** Education (JoHLSTE) which is ...
Horwath Asia Pacific : Hotel, **Tourism** and **Leisure** Consulting ...
altis.ac.uk/browse/cabi/ 1a009b81dfa8f2edcd0e78a442abb799.page7.html - 24k - Cached - Similar pages

(3) Portal de Biblioteca :: Universidad del Este
Journal of **Hospitality** and **Leisure** Marketing **Journal** of **Hospitality** & **Tourism** Research ...
Employment Review **Employment Recruitment** and Retention ...
www.suagm.edu/SUAGM/une/portal_biblioteca/ biblio_revistas_impresas.htm - 51k - Cached - Similar pages

(4) Retail Sales and **Hospitality** Jobs Xpress **Recruitment**
Professional **Hospitality**, **Leisure** & **Tourism** Body Scottish branch ... The **Recruitment** and **Employment** Confederation (REC) is the UK association that ...
www.xpressrecruitment.com/links.asp - 50k - Cached - Similar pages

(5) **hospitality | HOSPITALITY HOSPITALITY** NEWSHospitality News ...
Hlst ltsn JoHLSTE Online The **Journal** of **Hospitality Leisure** Sport & **Tourism** Education JoHLSTE Go to **Hospitality Leisure** Sport and **Tourism** Network Homepage ...
www.free-business-webdirectory.com/ business/hospitality/ - 81k - Cached - Similar pages

(6) Job Search Resources - Cornell Hotel School
Hospitality Jobs Online - Provides internet recruiting services to ... **Hospitality** Online Jobs - **Hospitality**, **tourism**, and travel industry **employment** and ...
www.hotelschool.cornell.edu/links/hslinks.html?scid=27&name=General+Hospitality+and+Business +Resource... - 18k - Cached - Similar pages

(7) **Hospitality**, **Leisure**, Sport and **Tourism** Network
... its **recruitment** of students to part time work for its clients, **employers** in ... The HLSTN is indebted to the ...
www.hlst.heacademy.ac.uk/HAVE/report_june03.html - 29k - Cached - Similar pages

(8) **Hospitality**, **Leisure**, Sport and **Tourism** Network
Events · **Journal** of **Hospitality**, **Leisure**, Sport, and **Tourism** Education · What's ... **Employers** in the New Graduate Labour Market: **recruiting** from a wider ...
www.hlst.heacademy.ac.uk/resources/employability.html - 60k - Cached - Similar pages

[More results from www.hlst.heacademy.ac.uk]

(9) ILAM - Careers guidance for the **leisure** industry
Journal of **Hospitality**, **Leisure**, Sport and **Tourism** Education (JoHLSTE) ... staff development and recruitment organisation for local government **employees** ...
www.ilam.co.uk/pd-careers.asp - 46k - Cached - Similar pages

(10) **Hospitality**/Hotel, Restaurant Administration
Human Resources: Human Resource Management, **Recruiting** and Training, ... Self-employment/Freelance Newspapers, magazines, and trade **journals Tour** operators ...
www.asu.edu/studentaffairs/career/ Students/ChoosingAMajor/html/hotelrest.htm - 14k - Cached - Similar pages

Understanding abbreviations and acronyms

An **abbreviation** is a shorter version of something. For example, PC /piːsiː/ is an abbreviation for *personal computer*.

An **acronym** is similar to an abbreviation, but it is pronounced as a word. For example, ALVA /ˈælvə/ is the *Association of Leading Visitor Attractions*.

We normally write an abbreviation or acronym with **capital letters**, although the full words have lower case letters.

We **pronounce** the vowel letters in **abbreviations** in this way:

A	/eɪ/
E	/iː/
I	/aɪ/
O	/əʊ/
U	/juː/

We normally **pronounce** the vowel letters in **acronyms** in this way:

A	/æ/
E	/e/
I	/ɪ/
O	/ɒ/
U	/ʌ/

Common suffixes

Suffixes for verbs

There are some common verb suffixes.

Examples:

~ize	*computerize*
~ify	*identify*
~ate	*accommodate*

When you learn a new noun or adjective, find out how you can make it into a verb.

Suffixes for nouns

There are many suffixes for nouns. But verbs ending in *~ize*, *~ify* and *~ate* form nouns with *~ation*.

Examples:

Verb	Noun	
~ize	*~ization*	*computerization*
~ify	*~ification*	*identification*
~ate	*~ation*	*accommodation*

Developing ideas in a paragraph

Introducing the topic

In a text, a new paragraph signals the start of a **new topic**. The topic is given in the **topic sentence**, which is at or near the beginning of the paragraph. The topic sentence gives the topic, and also makes a **comment** about the topic.

Example:
Tourism-related employment is different from many other employment sectors.

Here *tourism-related employment* is the **topic**. The **comment** is that it *is different from many other employment sectors*.

The sentences that follow then expand or explain the topic sentence.

Example:
For one thing, tourism is a highly mobile industry.

Developing the topic

A paragraph is normally about the same basic topic (the 'unity principle'). However, often the ideas **develop** beyond the comment in the topic sentence.

Example:
Moreover, … a large number of people … work on a part-time basis.

This sentence introduces a development extending employment in the tourism industry from full-time to part-time. Topic developments may be contrasts, comments, additional information, etc.

Development is often shown by:
• a **discourse marker**: *but, however,* etc.
• a **stance marker**: *unfortunately, sadly, needless to say,* etc.

Discourse markers generally make a connection between the previous information and what comes next. They mainly introduce contrasts or additional information.

Stance markers show the **attitude** of the writer to the information, i.e., whether he/she is surprised, pleased, unhappy, etc. about the information.

Recording and reporting findings

When you do research, record information about the source. Refer to the source when you report your findings.

Examples:
As Drucker suggests in his 2001 article in The Economist, …
According to Kotler, Bowen and Makens in their book Marketing for Hospitality and Tourism (2006), …
Morrison (2002) states that …
As the writer of the article on The Guardian Unlimited (March 4, 2008) says, …

You should give the full information about the source in your reference list or bibliography. For more information about this, see Unit 10 *Skills bank*.

5 TOURISM MARKETING

A Look at the photographs on the opposite page.

1 Name the types of resort you see. What do they specialize in? What sort of people visit each type?

2 In what way are resorts different from, for instance, hotels?

B Study the words in box a.

1 Make pairs with similar meanings.

2 What part of speech is each word?

> **a**
>
> activity   advertising   aim   business   buy   company
> consumer   customer   main   meet   needs   principal
> promotion   purchase   requirements   retail outlet
> satisfy   shop   target   task

C Study the Hadford University handout on this page.

1 Find a word in box a for each blue word. Change the form if necessary.

2 Find another word in the handout for each red word.

D Study the words in box b.

1 Find pairs of opposites.

2 Add more words to make a set.

3 Give a name to each word set.

> **b**
>
> careful   conventional   elderly   female   impulsive
> low-income   male   manual   married   professional
> single   trendy   wealthy   young

E Work with a partner.

1 Choose a resort on the opposite page. Describe its target market. Use words from box b and others.

2 Your partner should guess which resort you are talking about.

F Study Figure 1 on the opposite page.

1 What does the graph show?

2 What happened to the market shares?

3 Which company outperformed the others? Why?

4 Which company lost the biggest market share? Why?

G Study the description of Figure 2 on this page. Write one or two words in each space.

Faculty: Tourism and Hospitality

Lecture: Introduction to tourism marketing

Marketing of tourism is not ...

● ... the same as advertising. This is only a small part of marketing.

● ... just about selling. There are many other related activities which are involved.

So what is it?

There are four main aspects, known as the 'marketing mix' – also called the 'Four Ps' – to which companies must pay attention.

1 The **Product** – must meet the needs of the consumers.

2 **Promotion** – there are several methods of promoting a product, including advertising, special offers, mailing and sponsorship.

3 The **Price** – this depends on the financial objectives as well as the kind of consumer you aim at.

4 The **Place** – where do people buy the products? This concerns both means of distribution and type of retail outlet.

Figure 2 shows changes _____ sales _____ resort holidays _____ the year 2006/7. There was a _____ of 15% _____ sales of eco-resorts while sales _____ lake resort holidays went down _____ 10%. Ski holidays showed a 17% _____ in sales, and beach resort sales also _____. However, health resort sales _____ a 10% _____ .

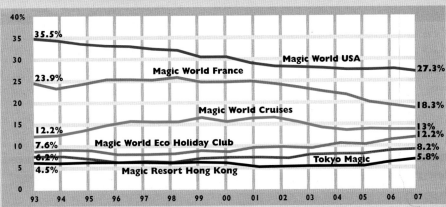

Figure 1:

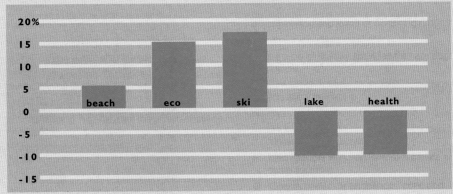

Figure 2: *Resort % sales growth 2006–2007*

A You are going to hear a lecture about key concepts in tourism marketing.

   1 Look at the lecture slides. What will the lecturer talk about? Make a list of points.

   2 Put your points in a logical order.

B 🎧 Listen to Part 1 of the lecture. How will the lecture be organized? Number these topics.

   • market research   ____

   • definition of marketing   ____

   • types of market   ____

   • importance of marketing   ____

   • basic characteristics of markets ____

C Study the topics in Exercise B.

   1 Make a list of words associated with each topic.

   2 Use the words to describe Slides 1–4.

   3 What is a good way to make notes?

   4 Make an outline for your notes.

D 🎧 Listen to Part 2 of the lecture.

   1 Add information to your outline notes.

   2 Which of the topics in Exercise B are discussed? In what order?

   3 What are theme park resorts an example of?

   4 What has Disney done when it comes to accommodation in their resorts?

E 🎧 Listen to Part 3 of the lecture. Make notes.

   1 Which topics in Exercise B are mentioned?

   2 Which topic has not been mentioned?

   3 Give two ways in which we can measure market size.

   4 What is the lecturer talking about when she loses her place?

   5 Describe two types of market.

F Match synonyms from the lecture.

   1 key concept   identify

   2 know, find out   a narrow category

   3 market leader   accurate data

   4 aimed at   important point

   5 a small part   top-selling brand

   6 good information   suitable for

Top 10 US theme and amusement parks by estimated attendance:	
1	Walt Disney World's Magic Kingdom
2	Disneyland
3	Epcot
4	Disney-MGM Studios
5	Disney's Animal Kingdom
6	Universal Studios Florida
7	Disney's California Adventure
8	Universal's Islands of Adventure
9	SeaWorld Florida
10	Universal Studios Hollywood

Slide 1

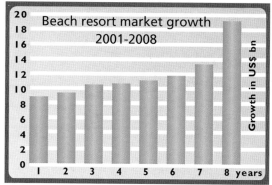

Your home away from home

luxury apartments
* family-friendly accommodation

Slide 2

Beach resort market growth 2001-2008

Growth in US$ bn

Slide 3

LUXO

Holidays for the over 50s

Slide 4

5.3 Extending skills
note-taking symbols • stress within words • lecture language

A Look at the student notes on the right. They are from the lecture in Lesson 2.

1 What do the symbols and abbreviations mean?

2 The notes contain some mistakes. Find and correct them.

3 Make the corrected notes into a spidergram.

B 🎧 Listen to the final part of the lecture (Part 4).

1 Complete your notes.

2 Why does the lecture have to stop?

3 What is the research task?

C 🎧 Listen to some stressed syllables. Identify the word below in each case. Number each word.

Example: You hear: *1 sem* /sem/

You write:

analyse	___	characteristics	___
anticipate	___	identify	___
assignment	___	overview	___
category	___	qualitative	___

seminar _/_

strategy ___

successful ___

variety ___

D Study the extract from the lecture on the right.

1 Think of one word for each space.

2 🎧 Listen and check your ideas.

3 Match words or phrases from the blue box below with each word or phrase from the lecture.

4 Think of other words or phrases with similar meanings.

> as I was saying   basically   clearly   crucial
> in fact   in other words   obviously
> of course   possibly   probably
> some people say   that is to say
> we can see that

E Discuss the research task set by the lecturer.

1 What kind of information should you find?

2 What do you already know?

3 Where can you find more information?

---

3) basic characteristics of markets

  (i) size

    e.g., beach resort market (UK)

    • c. $12 m

    • > 2 bn hols.

  (ii) market share (newest brand = market leader)

4) types of market

  e.g.,

  (i) beach/ski resort = niche market

  (ii) Over 50s hols. = mass market

_____ , marketing is _____ the most important aspect of management. So, *it* _____ *that* marketing must ensure that a business can satisfy customers' needs. *What I* _____ *is*, they anticipate consumers' requirements. _____ , successful marketing is about having accurate data. Anyway, er … to *return to the main* _____ , it's _____ to identify basic characteristics of the market. _____ , it is the aim of all companies to become the market leader.

A Study Figure 1 on the opposite page.

   1 What does it show?

   2 Where do you think the information has come from?

B 🎧 Listen to some extracts from a seminar about market mapping.

   1 What is wrong with the contribution of the last speaker in each case? Choose from the following:

- it is irrelevant
- the student interrupts
- the student doesn't contribute anything to the discussion
- it is not polite
- the student doesn't explain the relevance

   2 What exactly does the student say, in each case?

   3 What should the student say or do, in each case?

C 🎧 Listen to some more extracts from the same seminar.

   1 How does the second speaker make an effective contribution in each case? Choose from the following:

- by making clear how the point is relevant
- by bringing in another speaker
- by asking for clarification
- by paraphrasing to check understanding
- by giving specific examples to help explain a point

   2 What exactly does the student say, in each case?

   3 What other ways do you know of saying the same things?

D Make a table of **Do's** (helpful ways) and **Don't**s (unhelpful ways) of contributing to seminar discussions.

Do's	Don'ts
ask politely for information	demand information from other students

E Work in groups.

   1 Study the golf product group on the opposite page.

   2 Discuss how you put these products on a market map. Make sure you can justify your decision.

   3 Conduct a seminar. One or two people should act as observers.

F Report on your discussion and present your market map, giving reasons for your decisions.

G Work in groups of four. Each person should research the advantages and disadvantages of one of the four main types of market research. Report back to the group and ask other people about their research.

- Student A: find out about *secondary research* (information on page 104)
- Student B: find out about *primary research* (information on page 103)
- Student C: find out about *quantitative research* (information on page 104)
- Student D: find out about *qualitative research* (information on page 103)

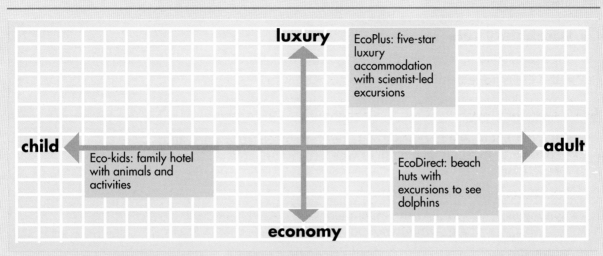

Figure 1: *Market map for eco-resorts*

Figure 2: *Golfing holidays*

Vocabulary sets

It is a good idea to learn words which go together. Why?

- It is easier to remember the words.
- You will have alternative words to use when paraphrasing research findings.
- It is not good style to repeat the same word often, so writers, and sometimes speakers, make use of words from the same set to avoid repetition.

You can create a vocabulary set with:

synonyms	words with similar meanings, e.g., *products/goods/items*
antonyms	words with opposite meanings, e.g., *male/female*
hypernyms	a general word for a set of words, e.g., *vehicle = car, truck, lorry*, etc.
word families	e.g., *young, teenage, in his/her 20s, middle-aged, old*

Describing trends

You can use a variety of phrases to discuss trends and statistics.

Examples:

Go up	No change	Go down	Adverbs
rise	*stay the same*	*fall*	*slightly*
increase	*remain at …*	*decrease*	*gradually*
grow	*doesn't change*	*decline*	*steadily*
improve	*is unchanged*	*worsen*	*significantly*
soar		*drop*	*sharply*
		plunge	*dramatically*
		plummet	

Stance

Speakers often use certain words and phrases to show how they feel about what they are saying.
Common stance words are:

In many cases, different stance words and phrases are used in spoken and written language.

adverbs	*arguably* *naturally* *sadly*
phrases	*of course, …* *it's essential to/that …* *we might say that …*

Spoken	Written
another thing	*additionally*
it seems	*evidently*
unfortunately	*regrettably*
believe	*contend*

Signpost language in a lecture

At the beginning of a lecture, a speaker will usually outline the talk.
To help listeners understand the order of topics, the speaker will use
phrases such as:

To start with I'll talk about …
Then I'll discuss …
After that, we'll look at …
I'll finish by giving a summary of …

During the lecture, the speaker may:

indicate a new topic	*Moving on (from this) …*
say the same thing in a different way	*What I mean is, …* *That is to say, …* *To put it another way, …*
return to the main point	*Where was I? Oh, yes.* *To return to the main point …* *As I was saying …*

Seminar language

The discussion leader may:

ask for information	*What did you learn about …?* *Can you explain …?* *Can you tell me a bit more about …?*
ask for opinions	*What do you make of …?* *This is interesting, isn't it?*
bring in other speakers	*What do you think, Majed?*

Participants should:

be polite when disagreeing	*Actually, I don't quite agree …*
make relevant contributions	*That reminds me …*
give examples to explain a point	*I can give an example of that.*

Participants may:

ask for clarification	*Could you say more about …?*
paraphrase to check understanding	*So what you're saying is …*
refer back to establish relevance	*Just going back to …*

6 THE BUSINESS OF EVENTS TOURISM

6.1 Vocabulary — paraphrasing at sentence level

A Study the words in the blue box.

1 Copy and complete the table. Put the words in one or more boxes, in each case.

2 Add or take away affixes to make words for the empty boxes. (Some will not be possible.)

3 Find a synonym for each word.

4 Group the words in the blue box according to their stress pattern.

B Study Figure 1 on the opposite page. Discuss these questions.

1 What does the diagram show?

2 Give a short description of each phase of the life cycle of an annual festival.

C Student A has written about the life cycle of an event, but there are some mistakes. Change the blue words, so the sentences are true.

D Student B has also written about the life cycle of an event. Match each sentence with a corrected sentence from Exercise C.

E Look at Figures 2 and 3 on the opposite page. Which of the two life cycles are most likely for the following events? Why?

- the 2000 UK millennium celebrations
- the annual Sydney writers' festival

F Choose one of these events.

- an art exhibition
- an annual Star Trek convention
- the launch of a seaside resort in a country just out of war

1 Draw its probable event life cycle.

2 Write some sentences to describe the life cycle of your event.

3 Give your sentences to your partner. Your partner should try to guess which event you have described.

4 Rewrite your partner's sentences with the same meaning.

---

attend   celebration   complicated
considerable   corporate
event   investment   involve
opt   predict   provide   significant
value   venture   virtual

Noun	Verb	Adjective
	attend	

Student A

1 Cash flow is positive during the development phase of an event.

2 In the development phase of an event, costs are high.

3 Cash flow becomes positive in the growth phase.

4 Decreasing attendance means that costs per visitor are reduced.

5 Attendance is at its peak once the market has declined.

6 Attendance may start to rise when the market reaches saturation.

Student B

a It is not until the maturity phase is reached that cash flow is no longer negative.

b Peak attendance figures are achieved at the maturity phase.

c While the event is being designed and trialled, there are many expenses but no income.

d There may be a reduction in business if there are too many competitors.

e It costs a lot to produce each event early in the cycle.

f As ticket sales go up, each visitor will cost the events organizers less money.

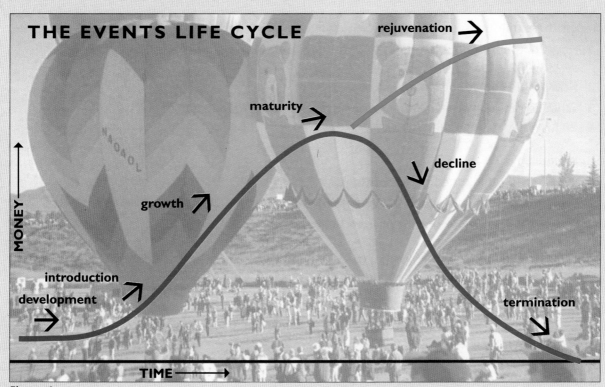

Figure 1

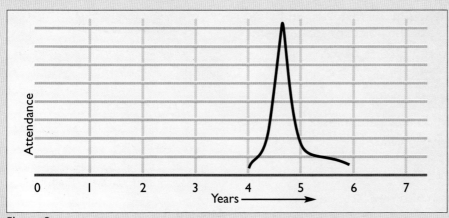

Figure 2

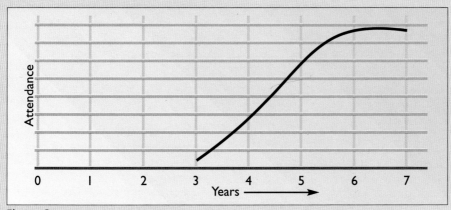

Figure 3

A Discuss these questions.

1 How do 'events' relate to tourism? What type of tourism events can you think of? List and order them according to popularity.

2 How would you define 'tourist' in this context?

3 What aspects do you think are most important in the organization of such events?

B Study Figure 1.

1 What do you think the figure represents?

2 What title would you give this figure?

3 Where does research come into events management?

C Look at the illustrations, the title, the introduction and the first sentence of each paragraph on the opposite page. What will the text be about?

D Using your ideas from Exercises A, B and C above, write some research questions.

E Read the text. Does it answer your questions?

F Study the highlighted sentences in the text. Find and underline the subject, verb and the object or complement in each sentence.
See Skills bank

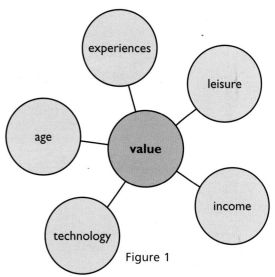

Figure 1

G Two students paraphrased parts of the text.

1 Which parts of the text do they paraphrase?

2 Which paraphrase is better? Why?

Student A

1 Festivals are major events which are attended by large groups of people; they are highly complex from an organizational point of view, and are expensive to put on.

2 The demand for professional events managers' has increased as the number of big events has grown.

3 There is no limit to what tourism events can look like, and they can be virtual as well as real.

4 One theory says that ageing contributes to the growth of events tourism.

5 Apart from age and technology, income and increased leisure time contribute to this growth as well.

Student B

1 Festivals are huge events, with many people involved, complicated logistics, management and considerable investment.

2 The tourism sector has seen a significant increase in these unique mega ventures, creating the need for professional events managers.

3 The rule of thumb seems to be that events can be as complicated as people can afford. Events can be real or virtual.

4 Theories claim that big events provide a forum for such celebrations as people age.

5 Added to ageing and technology, increased income and leisure time also form a recipe for growth in events tourism.

H Work in groups. Each group should write a paraphrase of a different part of the text.
See Vocabulary bank

The event of your life?

Festivals are the most popular tourist events. They are huge, with hundreds if not thousands of people active and involved, complicated logistics, stressful management and considerable investment.

If you are a young adult, the chances are that you belong to the large group of people who have visited a music festival at one point during their teen years. Perhaps you are a lover of festivals and go to many every year. Perhaps you are one of many people who have occasionally participated in or attended a sports festival, ranging from a regional competition to the Olympic Games. In America alone, more than 40,000 festivals are organized every year, including food festivals, music festivals and religious festivals. Some are one-off events; others are ongoing.

The organization of events is big business and has a direct relationship with tourism. In fact, although events attract some 'locals', most are organized to draw people in from outside the area, either internal tourists or visitors from abroad. In the 20th century, there was a boom in world fairs and major sports events. Millennium celebrations and live music events provided a further boost to events tourism. The tourism sector has seen a significant increase in the size, scope, length and visibility of these unique ventures, known as 'hallmark' or 'mega' events, creating the growing need for professional events managers.

Even though events organization is a professional skill, there do not seem to be hard and fast rules. People participate in events as individuals, but companies, too, provide corporate events tourism by organizing trips, themed weekends and festivals for their personnel and families. The rule of thumb seems to be that events can be as outrageous or complicated as money can buy. And nowadays, events can even be virtual: millions of people participate in highly organized events on the Internet every day.

Quite a few theories have been put forward as to why events tourism is so popular. There is one theory (Goldblatt, 2000) which claims that there is significantly more to celebrate as the Earth's population ages, and big events provide a forum for such celebrations. Another theory is that, with the huge advances in technology of the last few decades, people are seeking experiences that go beyond what they have experienced before, some say to balance the high-tech influences in their lives.

So what really attracts people to events? Researchers have found that participants feel they add value to their personal and work lives. In terms of tourism, there is a trend where people reduce the length of holidays and opt for shorter and more frequent breaks, during which they often attend festivals. It seems as if four factors play a role. We have already mentioned ageing and technology. Add to these increased income and more leisure time and you have a recipe for events tourism which increases the demand for events all around the world. This trend is expected to continue.

Researchers have already predicted interplanetary broadcasting events for the 2020s which, in the light of recent developments in space flight, may not seem such a remote idea anymore.

A Study the words in box a from Lesson 2.

  1 What part of speech are they in the text?

  2 Think of one or more words that have a similar meaning to each word.

> participate in   ongoing
> boost   put forward   claim   seek
> trend   reduce   frequent

B Complete the summary with words from Exercise A. Change the form or part of speech if necessary.

C Study the words in box b.

  1 What is each base word?

  2 How does the affix change the part of speech?

  3 What is the meaning in the text in Lesson 2?

> An increasing number of people
> _____ mega events. These
> events _____ tourism in an
> area. Researchers _____ that
> participants are _____ new
> experiences in our age of technology.
> Other theories have been _____
> which show that the _____ is
> for people to _____ the number
> of long holidays they have and opt for
> more _____ short breaks.
> Hallmark events seem to top the list of
> tourists' preferences. Some are one-off
> events, others are _____ .

D Study sentences A–E on the opposite page.

  1 Copy and complete Table 1. Put the parts of each sentence in the correct box.

  2 Rewrite the main part of each sentence, changing the verb from active to passive or passive to active.

E Look at the 'Other verbs' column in Table 1.

  1 How are the clauses linked to the main part of the sentence?

  2 In sentences A–C, what does each relative pronoun refer to?

  3 Make simpler versions of the original sentences.

> stressful   regional
> visibility   professional   themed
> outrageous   population   interplanetary

A Make one sentence for each box on the right, using the method given in red. Include the words in blue. Write the sentences as one paragraph.

> Vodafone made a deal with the Summadayze music festival in Australia and New Zealand.
> Vodafone sponsored the festival.
> relative, passive   In 2006

B Study the notes on the opposite page which a student made about a case study. Write up the case study.

  1 Divide the notes into sections to make suitable paragraphs.

  2 Decide which ideas are suitable topic sentences for the paragraphs.

  3 Make full sentences from the notes, joining ideas where possible, to make one continuous text.

> The stages displayed Vodafone's name.
> The entrance tickets displayed Vodafone's name.
> passive, ellipsis   In the deal

> People attending the festival had access to special mobile phone services.
> These services gave information about the bands performing.
> These services gave information about the latest gigs.
> relative, passive, ellipsis   In addition

> Vodafone created new added value.
> Vodafone attracted a new range of customers.
> participle   As a result

A   In the UK the name of the annual music festival which was previously known as Music on the Sea was changed to the International Shanty Festival.

B   Three of the many ways in which an event can be evaluated will be described here.

C   You can also post messages on the Internet blog, which is so useful that this benefit has played an important part in the rate at which this event has developed.

D   **As well as understanding its target audiences, an events management company must fully understand the qualities of its products.**

E   Having taken these steps as part of an integrated events management approach, the organizers saw a satisfactory increase in attendance.

Table 1: Breaking a complex sentence into constituent parts

	Main S	Main V	Main O/C	Other V + S/O/C	Adv. phrases
A	the name (of the annual music festival)	was changed	(to) the International Shanty Festival	which was known as Music on the Sea	In the UK; previously
B					

Marketing strategy in a mature market:

A case study - Organizing Fundays at the City Art Gallery

- art gallery operating in a small market - needs to maintain a competitive edge - how?
- good e.g. of this situation = City Art Gallery sponsorship programme
- analysis of figures → museum attendance low: market reached maturity
- gallery developed 2 major new activities:
  1) activities for families on Sunday afternoons - many attractions
  2) online gallery - pre/during/after visit - show all collection + many other features
- parents saw benefits quickly
- sharp increase in web hits → people get interested in gallery/activities
- → attendance up
- Sunday afternoon events - v.well attended
- after making changes, gallery did research:
  - attracted new (esp. younger) customers
  - kept existing customers
  - increased awareness of gallery
  - new activities = v. important for young visitors
- long-term issue = finance - how to keep events going?
- sponsorship = good marketing strategy
- family performance activities attracted interest of media
- Sunday Telegraph newspaper → aim: younger readership
- to keep ahead paper had to look at poss. extra benefits → attract existing + new readers
- deal made = Sunday Telegraph sponsored "Funday Afternoon Family Activities"
- arrangement = beneficial to both parties
- both gallery and newspaper achieved aims + created added value

Reporting findings

You cannot use another writer's words unless you directly quote. Instead, you must restate or **paraphrase**.

There are several useful ways to do this:

use a synonym of a word or phrase	costs ➜ expenses in the introduction phase ➜ early in the project
change negative to positive and vice versa	attendance declined ➜ attendance didn't increase
use a replacement subject	attendance may decline ➜ there may be a decline in attendance
change from active to passive or vice versa	the organizers can put on the event more cheaply ➜ the event can be put on more cheaply
change the order of information	in the introduction phase, unit costs are high ➜ it costs a lot to put on an event early in the life cycle

When reporting findings from one source, you should use all the methods above.

Example:

Original text	Cash flow is negative during the event's development phase.
Report	While the event is being designed and trialled, there are many expenses but no income.

Important

When paraphrasing, you should aim to make sure that 90% of the words you use are different from the original. It is not enough to change only a few vocabulary items: this will result in plagiarism.

Example:

Original text	If attendance starts to fall, does this indicate a decline?
Plagiarism	If sales drop, does this mean a decline?

Finding the main information

Sentences in academic and technical texts are often very long.

Example:
In terms of tourism, there is a trend where people looking for entertainment and relaxation considerably reduce the length of annual holidays and opt for shorter and more frequent breaks, during which they often attend festivals.

You often don't have to understand every word, but you must **identify the subject, the verb and the object,** if there is one.

For example, in the sentence above, we find:
subject = *people*
verb = *reduce/opt*
object = *holidays/breaks*

Remember!

You can remove any leading prepositional phrases at this point to help you find the subject, e.g., *In terms of tourism, ...*

You must then find **the main words which modify** the subject, the verb and the object or complement.

In the sentence above we find:
Which people? = those looking for entertainment and relaxation
How reduce? = considerably
What holidays? = annual ones

Ellipsis

Sometimes, if the meaning is clear, words are implied rather than actually given in the text.

Examples:
There are many strategies (which were) considered by such events companies.

Vodafone's name was displayed on the stage and (Vodafone's name was displayed) on the tickets.

7.1 Vocabulary

compound nouns • fixed phrases

A Study the words in box a.

1 Match nouns in column 1 with nouns in column 2 to make compound nouns.

2 Which word in each phrase has the strongest stress?

B Study the phrases in box b.

1 Complete each phrase with one word.

2 Is each phrase followed by:
- a noun (including gerund)?
- subject + verb?
- an infinitive?

3 What is each phrase used for?

C Look at pictures A–F on the opposite page showing the process of setting up the Goldorama Theme Park.

1 Put them in the correct order.

2 Describe what is happening at each stage.

D Study extracts A–F on the right from the Goldorama business plan.

1 Complete each sentence with a phrase from box b. Use each phrase once only.

2 Which extracts are probably from the finance section of the plan?

E Look at the Gantt chart on the opposite page. What does it show?

F Read the text under the Gantt chart. Match the phrases in box c with the highlighted phrases.

G Look at pictures 1–3 on the opposite page. Complete the Goldorama memo using phrases from Exercise B and box c.

a	1	2
	advertising	flow
	business	cycle
	capital	exposure
	cash	campaign
	life	industry
	service	investment
	theme	park
	TV	plan

b

as shown ...   as well ...   in addition ...
in order ...   in such a way ...   in the case ...
known ...   the end ...   the use ...

(A) _____ as completing technical specifications, investment companies will also want to know what events and shows the park intends to organize, and how the park plans to attract visitors.

(B) _____ to offering exciting rides, a theme park must also offer visitors shops and shows to complete their experience.

(C) _____ to satisfy the visitors, events in a theme park will, most importantly, have to entertain – education can be part of the experience but only _____ that visitors don't get bored.

(D) _____ in table 2 below, financing a theme park requires high capital investment.

(E) _____ of Goldorama Theme Park, the advertising campaign will begin six months before the park opens.

(F) Simulator rides are also _____ as virtual reality events; more and more parks offer these.

My recommendation is that the design _____ picture 1 should go into production. My opinion is_____ personal preference but also on _____ other points. Firstly,_____ maximize our visitor numbers we need to_____ the younger market. The_____ this market is important for the success of this theme park. _____ this design, the speed and challenge of the ride are very attractive for younger people. _____ this, the construction process is not complex.

c

a number of   a variety of
at the same time
bear in mind   based on   deal with
from the point of view of
the beginning of
the development of

Gantt chart: Developing a new theme park ride

	Week 1	Week 2	Week 3	Week 4	Week 5	Week 6	Week 7
Idea development							
Drawings of new designs							
Prototypes							
Evaluation of prototypes							
Approval of best design							
Production begins							

A Gantt chart is a useful planning tool, especially for project management. The chart makes it easy to handle a situation where different stages overlap. For example, this chart shows the evolution of a new theme park ride. The start of the process involves several designers making drawings. Then, using the drawings, prototypes of the rides are made. Simultaneously, the prototypes are evaluated by the company directors, who use various criteria to choose the best design.

A You are going to hear this lecture. Write three questions you would like answered.

B 🎧 Listen to Part 1 of the lecture.

  1 What is the lecturer going to talk about? Write **Y** (yes), **N** (no) or **NG** (not given).
- attracting and entertaining people   ___
- the history of theme parks   ___
- stages of development   ___
- making people aware of the park   ___
- current/future trends   ___
- theme parks and the environment   ___

  2 How does the lecturer define a theme park?

C 🎧 Listen to Part 2 of the lecture.

  1 Make notes in an appropriate form.

  2 What is another word for *corporate*?

  3 Were your questions in Exercise A answered?

D Match each phrase in the first column of the table on the right with the type of information that can follow.

E 🎧 Listen to Part 3 of the lecture.

  1 Makes notes on the information that comes after the phrases in Exercise D.

  2 Were your questions in Exercise A answered?

HADFORD *University*

Producing the experience

Lecture overview

- Theme parks and tourism
- Setting up a park – the process
- Marketing the venture
- Current/future trends

Fixed phrase	Followed by ...
1 What do I mean by ...?	a different way to think about the topic
2 As you can see, ...	an imaginary example
3 Looking at it another way, ...	a key statement or idea
4 In financial terms, ...	a concluding comment giving a result
5 Say ...	a comment about something visual
6 The point is ...	an explanation of a word or phrase
7 In this way ...	a general idea put into a financial context

---

F 🎧 Listen for sentences 1–4 in Part 4 of the lecture. Which sentence (**a** or **b**) follows in each case? Why?

  1 The amusement park market is mature.
    a In such a market, a few big players will own most of the parks around the world.
    b A few big players will own most of the parks around the world in such a market.

  2 There will always be the race for bigger and better parks.
    a Examples of this are better facilities, faster rides, the highest rollercoaster and the latest technology.
    b Better facilities, faster rides, the highest rollercoaster and the latest technology are examples of this.

  3 An ageing population means that parks need to offer entertainment that suits older visitors, too.
    a In developing your theme park, the important thing is to realize that it's the older people who are bringing their grandchildren along.
    b What's important to realize in developing your theme park is that it's the older people who are bringing their grandchildren along.

  4 Finally, theme parks have to be media savvy.
    a Now a park must be designed for television; this is different from 30 years ago.
    b What's different from, say, 30 years ago, is that now they must be designed for television ...

G This lecturer is not very well organized. What problems are there in the lecture?

7.3 Extending skills
stress within words • fixed phrases • giving sentences a special focus

A 🎧 Listen to some stressed syllables. Identify the word below in each case. Number each word.

Example:

You hear: *1 tin* /tɪn/   You write:

benefit	_____	financial	_____	population	_____
calculate	_____	ingredient	_____	resource	_____
continuous	_1_	manufacturing	_____	sequence	_____
entertainment	_____	maximize	_____	simultaneously	_____

B 🎧 Listen to the final part of the lecture from Lesson 2.

1 Complete the notes on the right by adding a symbol or abbreviation in each space.

2 What research task(s) are you asked to do?

C Study the phrases from the lecture in the blue box. For which of the following purposes did the lecturer use each phrase?

- to introduce a new topic
- to emphasize a major point
- to add points
- to finish a list
- to give an example
- to restate

D Rewrite these sentences to give a special focus. Begin with the words in brackets.

1 Walt Disney came up with the idea of starting a theme park. (It)

2 In 1853, the first amusement park was opened. (It)

3 The location of the park is very important for the whole business operation. (What)

4 Planning is complex because planning decisions are based on a wide variety of different factors. (The reason)

5 A good design plan shows what the park will look like when it is finished. (The advantage)

See Skills bank

E Choose one section of the lecture. Refer to your notes and give a spoken summary. Use the fixed phrases and ways of giving special focus that you have looked at.

F Work with a partner.

1 Make a Gantt chart for an activity, project or process.

2 Present your chart to another pair. Practise using fixed phrases and ways of giving special focus.

Future of theme parks

big theme parks _____ demand for other services (_____ hotels, restaurants, shops) _____ visitors need these facilities

best e.g. _____ Disney World (whole park 28,000 acres, Magic Kingdom 100 acres!)

Surrounding facilities, _____

– golf course
– hotel/other accom.
– retail centre
– cinemas
– concert halls
– restaurants
– shops

Summary

1 must have clear vision _____ know what you want (which theme _____ rides _____ shows _____ markets to focus on)

2 each step requires careful planning (economic analysis, management) theme parks _____ v. complex businesses

** make guests feel special _____ entertain them

---

etcetera
In other words, ...
Let's take ...
Let me put it another way.
Not to mention the fact that ...
Plus there's the fact that ...
The fact of the matter is, ...
You've probably heard of ...

A Look at the map on the opposite page.

  1 What does it show?

  2 Why does it show the information like that?

  3 Where does the information come from?

B 🎧 Listen to the first extract from a seminar about business location.

  1 What question will the students discuss?

  2 Why is Goldorama's decision surprising?

C 🎧 Listen to the second extract from the seminar. Are these sentences true or false?

  1 Bristol is a good location for tourists. ____

  2 Bristol is not an important town in the region. ____

  3 The speakers agree that Bristol is a good location for a new theme park. ____

  4 Higher entrance fees are not necessarily a bad thing. ____

  5 Costs are the main issue in choosing a business location. ____

I'd like to make two points. First, … ____

Can you expand on that? ____

The point is … ____

What's your second point? ____

My second point is that … ____

Yes, but … ____

I don't agree with that because … ____

Sorry, but who are we talking about, exactly? ____

We need to be clear here. ____

I'd just like to say that … ____

In what way? ____

What I'm trying to say is, … ____

Can you give me an example? ____

Look at it this way. ____

Absolutely. ____

D Study tasks **a–d** below and the phrases in the blue box.

  1 Write **a**, **b**, **c** or **d** next to each phrase in the box to show its use.

    a introducing

    b asking for clarification

    c agreeing/disagreeing

    d clarifying

  2 🎧 Listen to the second extract from the seminar again to check your answers.

E Work in groups of five. You are going to carry out the research task from Lesson 3, Exercise B.

  1 First, study the photos on the opposite page and think about the best theme for the park.

  2 Have a practice seminar in which you decide what the theme should be.

  3 Report to the class on your discussion, giving reasons for your decisions.

F Continue working in your groups.

  1 Each student should choose and research one of the following:
- determine the best location for your theme park
- design the park and list the events, rides and shows
- think up a marketing campaign

  2 Report your findings to the other students in your group, and explain your decisions. Convince your fellow students and come to a joint decision.

  3 Groups report back orally to the class. Use fixed phrases to ask for and give clarification.

G In your groups, list three things to do to develop the park further in the future.

News → Press → Press Releases → Press Release

Home | News | Pictures | Reviews | Records | Top 10 | Quiz | FAQs

Theme Park News

Press Release: Goldorama to build major theme park in Bristol

Recognizing fixed phrases from tourism and hospitality (1)

There are many fixed phrases in the field of tourism and hospitality.

Examples:

Phrase	Meaning in the discipline
amusement park	an outdoor entertainment location
theme park	an amusement park with a distinct theme
service industry	an industry that provides a service rather than a product
TV exposure	being seen on television
hotel accommodation	rooms and apartments for tourists in a hotel
retail development	the building of shops at tourist locations

Keep a list of fixed phrases used in tourism and remind yourself regularly of the meaning.

Recognizing fixed phrases from academic English (1)

There are also a large number of fixed phrases which are commonly used in academic English.

Examples:

Phrase	What comes next?
As we have seen …	a reminder of previous information
An important concept is …	one of the basic points underlying the topic
As you can see, …	a reference to an illustration OR a logical conclusion to previous information
As shown in …	a reference to a diagram or table
… in such a way that …	a result of something
In addition to (X, Y)	X = reminder of last point, Y = new point
As well as (X, Y)	X = reminder of last point, Y = new point
In the case of …	a reference to a particular topic or, more often, sub topic
At the same time, …	an action or idea which must be considered alongside another action or idea
… based on …	a piece of research, a theory, an idea
Bear in mind (that) …	key information which helps to explain (or limit in some way) previous information
The point is …	the basic information underlying an explanation
in order to (do X, Y)	X = objective, Y = necessary actions/conditions
In financial terms, …	the cost of something previously mentioned
In other words, …	the same information put in a different way
Looking at it another way, …	the same information put in a different way
In this way …	a result from previous information
Say …	an example
What do I mean by (X)?	an explanation of X

Make sure you know what kind of information comes next.

Skills bank

'Given' and 'new' information in sentences

In English, we can put important information at the beginning or at the end of a sentence. There are two types of important information.

1 Information which the listener or reader already knows, from general knowledge or from previous information in the text. This can be called 'given' information. It normally goes at the beginning of the sentence.

2 Information which is new in this text. This can be called 'new' information. It normally goes at the end of a sentence.

Example:
In Lesson 2, the lecturer is talking about the amusement park market, so the amusement park market in general = given information.

Given	New
The amusement park market	is mature.
In such a market,	a few big players will own most of the parks around the world.

Giving sentences a special focus

We sometimes change the normal word order to emphasize a particular point, e.g., a person, an object, a time.

Examples:

Normal sentence	Walt Disney invented the modern theme park in the 1950s.
Focusing on person	It was Walt Disney who invented …
Focusing on object	It was the modern theme park which Walt Disney invented …
Focusing on time	It was in the early 1950s that Walt Disney invented …

Introducing new information

We can use special structures to introduce a new topic.

Examples:
Amusement parks are my subject today.
→ **What I am going to talk about today is** amusement parks.

Planning is very important.
→ **What is very important is** planning.

Bad management causes these problems.
→ **The reason for these problems is** bad management.

Poor marketing leads to commercial failure.
→ **The result of poor marketing is** commercial failure.

Clarifying points

When we are speaking, we often have to clarify points. There are many expressions we can use.

Examples:
Let me put it another way …
Look at it this way …

What I'm trying to say is …
The point/thing is …

8 HOSPITALITY MARKETING

A Study the words and phrases in box a. What do they relate to?

a

advertising   direct mail
internal marketing   localization
word of mouth

B Study the diagram on the opposite page.

   1 What does the diagram illustrate? Describe the process.

   2 Which aspects of marketing are shown in the pictures?

b

expense   objective   opportunity
perception   staff   strategy
trade   turnover

C Look up each noun in box b in a dictionary.

   1 Is it countable, uncountable or both?

   2 What is its business/marketing meaning?

   3 What is a good synonym?

   4 What useful grammatical information can you find?

D Study the two lists of verbs in box c.

   1 Match the verbs with similar meanings.

   2 Make nouns from the verbs if possible.

c

achieve	profit
allocate (to)	reserve (for)
attract	go down
boost	see
decline	manage (to)
gain	appeal (to)
perceive	keep
retain	promote

E Look at the text about marketing on the right.

   1 How does the writer restate the heading (*Budget marketing*) in the first paragraph?

   2 Find synonyms for the blue words and phrases. Use a dictionary if necessary.

   3 Write a paraphrase of each sentence. Use:

     • your own synonyms

     • words from Exercises C and D

     • passives where possible

   Example:

   The perception that you can do without marketing altogether is false.

   → *It is incorrect to assume that marketing can be ignored.*

Budget marketing

Most small hospitality businesses are undercapitalized. Even if they have allocated funds to marketing, new owners often find that the actual expenses are much higher; they also often find that marketing is a great deal less effective than they had anticipated. Therefore, the use of strategies that reduce the cost of marketing can mean the difference between survival and collapse.

Usually, small business owners cannot call upon specialist external marketing support without having to pay costly fees. So the more they can use the skills of in-house staff, the less work they need to outsource, and the more cost-effective the marketing becomes.

The perception that you can do without marketing altogether is false.

F Study the information about the Hadford University *Tourism operations* course on the opposite page.

   1 Match the skills on the right (A–P) with the modules on the left.

   2 Which modules would you follow if you wanted to learn more about the marketing of tourism?

   3 Which modules would be relevant to a tourism operator that had noticed the problems in box d in their organization?

d

a brochure that is unclear
meals that take too long to prepare and serve
high staff turnover
double bookings
spending more than the business earns
frequent accidents

Marketing strategy

research

↓

analysis

↓

opportunities

↓

marketing mix

↓

product development

→

- sales strategy
- promotional material
- direct mail
- advertising
- public relations
- special promotions

HADFORD *University*

Hadford University's *Tourism operations* course offers the following modules:

Module	Skills
1 Tourism industry knowledge	A Deal with conflict situations
2 Workplace procedures	B Manage quality customer service
3 Tourism administration	C Source and present information
4 Information technology	D Develop and implement a business plan
5 Product information	E Receive and process reservations
6 Bookings and quotations	F Monitor work operations
7 Sales and marketing	G Manage projects
8 Workplace safety	H Provide on-site event management services
9 Event management	I Develop and manage marketing strategies
10 Workplace operations	J Implement workplace health, safety and security procedures
11 Business development	K Plan and manage meetings
12 Financial management	L Manage finances within a budget
13 Project management	M Develop and update local knowledge
14 Leadership	N Integrate technology into the event management process
15 Risk management	O Establish and maintain a safe and secure workplace
16 Customer service	P Access and interpret product information

A Look at the names for hospitality outlets in the blue box.

1 What type of marketing process is most likely to be successful for each product? Give examples.

2 What could go wrong in the marketing process in each case?

B Look at the four essay types on the right.

1 What should the writer do in each type?

2 Match each essay type with one of the questions below the slide (A–D).

3 What topics should be covered in each essay question?

C Read the title of the text on the opposite page and the first sentence of each paragraph.

1 What will the text be about?

2 Choose one of the essay questions on the right (A–D). Write four research questions which will help you to find information for your essay.

D Read the text.

1 Find out whether there is information for your essay question in the text and make notes in your own words.

2 Work with another person who has chosen the same essay question as you. Compare your notes.

E Study the highlighted sentences in the text.

1 What grammatical feature do these sentences share?

2 Underline the passive verb forms in each sentence.

3 Rewrite each sentence in an active form.

Example:

Marketing is often considered to be 'just' advertising and selling …

→ *People often consider marketing to be just advertising and selling …*

F Study the table on the right.

1 Match each word or phrase with its meaning.

2 Underline the words or phrases in the text which the writer uses to give the definitions.

See Vocabulary bank

a casino   an eco-resort
a gourmet restaurant
a health spa   a local café

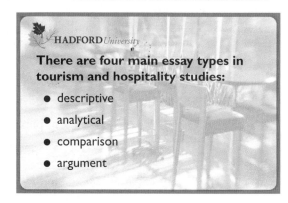

HADFORD *University*

There are four main essay types in tourism and hospitality studies:

● descriptive

● analytical

● comparison

● argument

(A) What are the best marketing tools for a hospitality business and what are their advantages and disadvantages?

(B) 'Hospitality is a service industry dealing in intangible goods. Therefore marketing must focus on experience.' To what extent do you agree with this statement?

(C) Explain why there are three distinctly different 'worlds' within the hospitality industry and why it is difficult in a hospitality career to cross over from one to the other.

(D) What are the basic components that make up tourism and hospitality products or services? Describe one or two products or services that you know which show evidence of these.

Word/phrase	Meaning
1 localization	addressed to clients outside the organization
2 intangible	decline
3 outlet	embedding services and products in the local setting
4 negative growth	place of retail business
5 external marketing	the service and sales skills of people within the company
6 internal marketing	you cannot see it/them

Finding your way in hospitality marketing

The hospitality industry, whether corporate, government or retail, is important for the economies of many countries in an age where travel is easy and the world becomes smaller every day. Businesses have known for a long time that their success is increased by good marketing; but misconceptions about marketing are widespread.

Marketing is often considered to be 'just' advertising and selling of attractions, transport, accommodation and entertainment. Of course it is much more, and includes the development of services, distribution, pricing, and also localization, which involves ensuring that services and products are embedded in the local setting. Through marketing, the right product or service is matched to the right market or people. As hospitality is a service industry, its main products are intangible, that is, you cannot see them. This means that businesses must consider improvement of the overall experience, including customer service and staffing. Companies should use a marketing system in which these aspects are continuously reviewed. Efficiency in marketing is required for this.

Let's focus on restaurants specifically. In this area, government hospitality may not be sales-driven enough, corporate hospitality may be subject to heavy competition, and there may simply be too many retail businesses, but the mix of people, systems and career paths is relevant to all sectors (although differing cultures may make it hard to cross from one to the other).

Not many catering organizations generate the turnover that is necessary to support the hiring of specialist staff or the funds to retain an external consultant to attend to their marketing for them. The majority of small business owners have to take the initiative themselves. One of the basic objectives of marketing is to attract new customers. Another is to repeat trade from customers so that the business can reach operational capacity. Visitor numbers may be insufficient to justify the expense of opening your outlet (place of retail business). What alternatives do operators have?

If an operator decides to build up their trade, there are certain matters which should be addressed before they begin. It is one thing acquiring new customers; it is, however, entirely different getting them to spend their money. Firstly, it is important to establish whether the present customer service is of a high enough standard to gain new customers by word of mouth. If not, there is no point in investing to attract new trade until there is certainty the operation is going to retain it. Secondly, the question must be asked whether the operator and staff are properly trained to make the most of sales opportunities when new customers present themselves. It is clear that these questions are now being addressed by the majority of hospitality operators.

According to research, there are two main ways to boost income. Operators can either increase customer numbers by marketing, or they can try to increase the average amount they take from each customer. Another option could be to increase prices, but most entrepreneurs do not consider this a workable option. They often see it as a last resort. If a business is showing negative growth or decline, while its operators are investing in marketing, it is clear that it must be losing customers.

To attract more customers, both external and internal marketing should be applied. External marketing is addressed to clients outside your organization. Examples are advertising, special promotions and direct mail. Simultaneously, operators should develop internal marketing – service and sales skills. The distinction between the two is very important, for without good internal marketing, any campaign to attract new customers is bound to lead to disappointing results.

Research has shown that it does not matter greatly what operators and staff think of their own business because customer perception is all there is in marketing. Customers will view any service in what Tom Peters described as 'their idiosyncratic and irrational way'. Excellent quality, above average service, consistency and the perception of value for money – that's what it's all about. If these conditions are fulfilled, research (as well as our own personal experience) has shown that growth will come naturally. Marketing is all about managing perceptions.

A Find the words in the box in the text in Lesson 2 (page 65).

  1 What part of speech is each word?

  2 Think of another word which could be used in place of the word in the text. Use your dictionary if necessary.

> misconception   retain   attend (to)
> objective   justify   establish
> gain   properly   consistency

B Study sentences A–D on the right.

  1 Identify the dependent clause.

  2 Copy the table under the sentences and write the parts of each dependent clause in the table.

  3 Rewrite the sentence using an active construction.

  Example:

  A Areas which companies have to consider incude customer service and staffing.

| A | Areas which have to be considered by companies include customer service and staffing. |

| B | Hospitality businesses have known for a long time that their success is increased by good marketing. |

| C | Companies should use a marketing system in which all these aspects are checked. |

| D | It is clear that this question is now being addressed by the majority of hospitality operators. |

C Read the essay plans and extracts on the opposite page.

  1 Match each plan with an essay title in Lesson 2.

  2 Which essay is each extract from?

  3 Which part of the plan is each extract from?

Subject	Verb	By whom/what
(areas) which	have to be considered	by companies

D Work with a partner.

  1 Write another paragraph for one of the plans.

  2 Exchange paragraphs with another pair. Can they identify where it comes from?

A Make complete sentences from these notes. Add words as necessary.

A through marketing – right product or service – matched – market or people

B tourism – service industry – main products – recreational experiences and hospitality – intangible

C basic objective – marketing – attract – new customers – also – repeat trade – existing customers – reach – operational capacity

D if – operator – decide – build up – business – some matters – address – at start

E operators – increase – customer numbers – marketing – or – try to increase – average amount – take – from each customer

F if – conditions – fulfil – research – personal experience – show – growth – follow

B Imagine you have been asked to write the essay titled: 'What are the best marketing tools for a local hospitality business and what are their advantages and disadvantages?' What would be the main topic for each paragraph of the essay: introduction / definition / advantages / disadvantages / conclusion?

C Look at the essay question on the right.

  1 What kind of essay is this?

  2 Do some research and make an essay plan.

  3 Write the essay.

> Emma Jones ran a business on a very popular campsite in France. She provided childcare and children's activities so parents could relax and spend time together. She advertised on the campsite's public notice-board and on their website. However, although Emma's services were very popular, the business ran into problems. She could not retain competent and motivated staff and so she lost business. What were the possible shortcomings of Emma's marketing activities?

Essay plans

A

1 Introduction: three different worlds in the hospitality industry

2 List worlds: government, corporate, retail

3 Define differences: people, values, systems management, problems, career paths

4 Give examples: hospital canteens, specialized (large) hospitality companies, small restaurants

5 Compare/analyse:
   a government: not sales-driven, bureaucratic, can be inefficient (⟶ outsourcing)

   b corporate: top-heavy management, heavy competition

   c small business: too many businesses, not enough customers, long working hours

6 Cross-over issues: management of each requires different skills, cultural differences require different attitudes, `grass is greener on other side' attitudes, research shows it's hard

7 Conclusion: leaping from the frying pan into the fire?

B

1 Introduction: What do tourism & hospitality products and services really consist of? Importance of understanding this question.

2 List basic components: attractions, entertainment, transport and accommodation

3 Further basic components: services, distribution and pricing

4 Key additional component: the overall customer experience

5 Company A: description of their product(s) / service(s)

6 Company B: description of their product(s) / service(s)

7 Conclusion: tourism and hospitality products consist of several basic components and must be marketed as a composite

Essay extracts

This is the third component in the tourism and hospitality product. It covers transportation to the attraction, and also proximity to a sufficiently large population to make a market for the attraction. 'Proximity' should not be seen as physical distance. It can best be defined in terms of the time and the cost it will take to reach the attraction.

This sector differs from the other two in that traditionally it is not sales-driven. The culture can also be more bureaucratic. In the UK, it is decreasing steadily in size. Managers in this sector often believe that efficiency is best achieved through outsourcing to the private sector. The majority of managers do not seek to improve efficiency through internal changes. Research has shown that many managers find themselves under continual threat of privatization.

Understanding new words: using definitions

You will often find new words in academic texts. Sometimes you will not be able to understand the text unless you look the word up in a dictionary, but often a technical term will be defined or explained immediately or later in the text.

Look for these indicators:

is or *are*	*'Marketing' is basically about ...*
brackets	*... outlet (place of retail business).*
or	*At the end of the marketing process we have the marketing campaign or the activities carried out to promote ...*
which	*... localization, which involves ensuring that services and products are embedded in the local setting.*
a comma or dash (–) immediately after the word or phrase	*... internal marketing – service and sales skills.*
phrases such as *in other words* *that is*	*... the core activity of a business: that is, how the business does what it does. In other words, how a company manages its marketing.*

Remember!

When you write assignments, you may want to define words yourself. Learn to use the methods above to give variety to your written work.

Understanding direction verbs in essay titles

Special verbs called **direction verbs** are used in essay titles. Each direction verb indicates a type of essay. You must understand the meaning of these words so you can choose the correct writing plan.

Kind of essay	Direction verbs
Descriptive	*State ... Say ... Outline ... Describe ... Summarize ... What is/are ...?*
Analytical	*Analyse ... Explain ... Comment on ... Examine ... Give reasons for ... Why ...? How ...?*
Comparison/ evaluation	*Compare (and contrast) ... Distinguish between ... Evaluate ... What are the advantages and/or disadvantages of ...?*
Argument	*Discuss ... Consider ... (Critically) evaluate ... To what extent ...? How far ...?*

Choosing the correct writing plan

When you are given a written assignment, you must decide on the best writing plan before you begin to write the outline. Use key words in the essay title to help you choose – see *Vocabulary bank*.

Type of essay – content	Possible structure
Descriptive writing List **the most important points** of something: e.g., in a narrative, a list of key events in chronological order; a description of key ideas in a theory or from an article you have read. Summarize points in a logical order. **Example:** *What are the key features of marketing management?*	• introduction • point/event 1 • point/event 2 • point/event 3 • conclusion

Analytical writing
List the **important points** which **in your opinion** explain the situation.
Justify your opinion in each case.
Look behind the facts at the **how** and **why**, not just **what/who/when**.
Look for and question accepted ideas and assumptions.
Example:
Explain the rise in online bookings from a marketing perspective.
	• introduction
	• definitions
	• most important point:
	  example/evidence/reason 1
	  example/evidence/reason 2
	  etc.
	• next point:
	  example/evidence/reason 3
	  example/evidence/reason 4
	  etc.
	• conclusion

Comparison/evaluation Decide on and define the **aspects** to compare two subjects. You may use these aspects as the basis for paragraphing. Evaluate which aspect(s) is/are better or preferable and give reasons/criteria for your judgment. **Example:** *Compare marketing practices in America and Great Britain.*	• introduction • state and define aspects *Either*: • **aspect 1:** subject A v. B • **aspect 2:** subject A v. B *Or:* • **subject A:** aspect 1, 2, etc. • **subject B:** aspect 1, 2, etc. etc. • conclusion/evaluation
Argument writing **Analyse** and/or **evaluate**, then give your **opinion** in a **thesis statement** at the beginning or the end. Show awareness of difficulties and disagreements by mentioning counter-arguments. **Support** your opinion with evidence. **Example:** *'Bad internal marketing is demotivating for the workforce.' Discuss with reference to two or three companies.*	• **introduction: statement of issue** • **thesis statement giving opinion** • **define terms** • **point 1:** explain + evidence • **point 2:** explain + evidence etc. • **conclusion:** implications, etc. *Alternatively:* • **introduction: statement of issue** • **define terms** • **for:** point 1, 2, etc. • **against:** point 1, 2, etc. • **conclusion: statement of opinion**

9.1 Vocabulary   fixed phrases

A Match the words to make fixed phrases.

1	developing	resources
2	capital	planning
3	agent of	travel
4	natural	country
5	public	health
6	retail	resort
7	destination	city
8	budget	development
9	health	change

1	2
a	… start with
some	… people think
	on … other hand
many	to … extent
this	on … one hand
that	… real question is
	on … grounds that
the	in … case like this
to	in … sort of situation

B Study the words and phrases in the blue box.

1 Complete each phrase in column 2 with a word from column 1.

2 Which phrase can you use to:
- agree only partly with a point
- begin talking about several points
- compare two ideas
- focus on an important point
- give a reason for a point
- mention an idea
- talk about certain circumstances

C Look at pictures 1–6 and quotes A–F on the opposite page.

1 Match each picture with a quote.

2 What is each person's connection with tourism? What aspects of tourism are they interested in?

3 In the quotes, replace the words in italics with a phrase from Exercise B.

D Read the extract on this page from the Hadford University handout about tourism in developing countries.

1 Match the blue words in this extract with the definitions on the opposite page.

2 Use your dictionary to check words you do not know.

HADFORD *University*

… destination planning is important for the management of tourism. Players in the field have to realize that the resources of some destinations are limited and a large influx of people can have negative effects. A country that is not used to mainstream tourism will not have the infrastructure in place to deal with it. In this way, tourism can become a controversial agent of change, and in the long term may not be sustainable. It can often cause a culture clash which may adversely affect a country and its people, especially if the destination was very inaccessible before. The best tourism is based on a genuine interest in the country, its people and their values and beliefs. Tourists must understand that in countries with scarce resources and strong traditional roots the indigenous population will want to preserve their heritage. So, tourism policies need to be developed carefully, and always in cooperation with the community.

A 'Profits are up quite a lot this year. *When this happens* we usually give the staff a generous pay increase – but this year we want to fund the building of extra rooms.'

B 'There are so many interesting places to see in this country. *Firstly*, there are lots of historic sights, and then there are the nature reserves …'

C 'We feel that we are lost, and the spirits of our ancestors are unhappy. *But* everybody tells us we should be happy, because tourism brings us wealth.'

D '*They say that* the quality of tourism services is reasonably good here. I *don't* agree *completely*. My party wants to create a better infrastructure.

E 'At the moment, we make about 75 deliveries a week to the hotels in town. But *the important thing is* whether we can keep up with demand.'

F 'I'm shocked, *because* most people I talk to have no idea of the pressures that tourism development puts on the natural resources of this country.'

---

www.hadford.ac.uk/bank/def

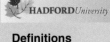
HADFORD *University*

Definitions

A a mass arrival

B plans of action drawn up by a government or business

C supplies that can be used when needed

D characteristics of a community which have grown over many generations

E the past and its traditions

F capable of continuing with minimal long-term effect on the environment

G free from hypocrisy or dishonesty, real

H hard to find

I something or someone that causes things to develop

J originating and living or occurring naturally in an area

K remote or unapproachable

L the type of holiday activities that are popular with many people

M thinking about how to develop a tourism area before you allow tourists in

N ideas that people firmly believe in

O the basic facilities and services needed for the functioning of a community

P when people with very different beliefs and lifestyles come together

Q keep in perfect or unchanged condition

A Study the slide on the right. What questions do you think the lecturer will answer?

B 🎧 Listen to Part 1 of the lecture.

1 Complete the *Notes* section below.

2 Complete the *Summary*.

3 Answer the *Review* questions.

4 Is the lecturer's story a 'real' story?

C 🎧 Create a blank Cornell diagram. Listen to Part 2 of the lecture.

1 Complete the *Notes* section.

2 Write some *Review* questions.

3 Complete the *Summary*.

4 Were your questions in Exercise A answered?

D 🎧 Study the phrases in column 1 of the blue box. Listen to some sentences from the lecture. Which type of information in column 2 follows each phrase?

HADFORD *University*

Tourism and culture (Lecture 1)

• Impact of industry on people

• Issues of people and infrastructure

• From a good start into a downward spiral

• Solutions: regulation

1	2
1 As we shall see …	a developing trend
2 In terms of …	information about a point the speaker will make later
3 It could be argued that …	
4 Research has shown that …	an aspect of a topic the speaker wants to focus on
5 Increasingly, we find that …	a statement the speaker agrees with
6 It's true to say that …	a conclusion
7 So it should be clear that …	an idea the speaker may or may not agree with

Review	Notes
	Impact of Tourism on _____
	The story = example of _____
Main issue is ... ?	Main issue: countries don't have basic _____
2 types of impact are ... ?	Two impacts: 1) tourism _____
	2) on local _____
Issues ... ?	Issues
1) spending?	1) spending $ in wrong places: _____ but not _____ infrastructure
2) infrastructure?	2) infrastructure improvements, e.g., _____ → spoil atmosphere
3) people?	3) influence on _____
Culture clash = ?	strengthening of local _____
	v. growth of _____

Summary

9.3 Extending skills
recognizing digressions • source references

A Study the words in box a.

1 Mark the stressed syllables.

2 🎧 Listen and check your answers.

3 Which is the odd one out in each group? Why?

B Study the phrases in box b.

1 Do you think the phrases show a digression (start or end) or a relevant point? Write **D** or **R**.

2 Look at the **D** phrases. Do they start or end the digression?

C 🎧 Listen to the final part of the lecture from Lesson 2.

1 Take notes using the Cornell system. Leave spaces if you miss information.

2 What topic does the lecturer mention that is different from the main subject?

3 Why does the lecturer mention this topic?

4 What is your research task?

5 Compare your notes in pairs. Fill in any blank spaces.

6 Complete the *Review* and *Summary* sections.

a

1 impact (n), influx, mainstream, preserve

2 acknowledge, consequence, heritage, influence

3 indigenous, infrastructure, publicity, sustainable

4 probably, generally, usually, financially

b

Now, where was I?

It's the first of these points that I'm going to focus on now ...

By the way, ...

So to get back to the topic ...

I have a story to tell you ...

If we move on now to ...

You don't need to take notes on this ...

Let's turn to ...

When we look at ... , we'll find ...

D 🎧 What information does the lecturer provide about sources? Listen to the extracts and complete the table below.

	Extract 1	Extract 2	Extract 3	Extract 4
Name of writer				
Title and date of source				
Location				
Type of reference				
Relevant to ...?				
Introducing phrase				

E Use your notes to write 75–100 words about tourism and culture.

F Work in groups. Study the five negative factors that may affect tourism in box c and find information on them and examples.

1 What kind of information will you need to find?

2 What ideas do you already have? Write some notes.

3 Where can you go to find more information?

c

local culture is affected

physical environment is damaged

explosive growth of low-status jobs

expressions of neo-colonialism

inappropriate conduct by foreigners

A Look at the words in the blue box. Identify their stress patterns.

> atmosphere   confidence   destination
> development   economy   effect
> employment   environmental   exploit (v)
> guidelines   monitor   positive   unique

B Work in pairs.

Student A: Think of good ways to take part in a seminar.

Student B: Think of bad ways to take part in a seminar.

C You are going to hear some students in a seminar. They have been asked to discuss the question: 'Why is culture important in tourism?'

   1 🎧 Listen to the seminar extracts. Put a ✓ for a good contribution and a ✗ for a poor one in the table below.

   2 Give reasons for your opinion.

	✓ / ✗	Reasons
Extract 1		
Extract 2		
Extract 3		
Extract 4		

D Study Figure 1. Which negative effects of tourism are shown in the photographs?

E Work in groups of three or four.

   1 Discuss and exchange the information you found for the topics in Lesson 3, Exercise F.

   2 Discuss how best to present this information.

   3 Present the result of your discussion to the class.

F You are going to take part in a seminar to discuss a new tourism project.

   1 Study the case information on the opposite page about Haru.

   2 Work in groups of six. Read your role card (see page 105) and prepare your role.

   3 In your group, discuss and agree how tourism should develop in Haru. Use the ideas, words and phrases from the unit.

   4 Finally, design a one-page brochure that explains your plans. Present the plans to the class.

Figure 1: *Some negative aspects of tourism*

Developing tourism in Haru

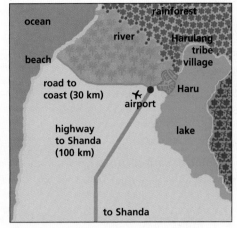

Haru is a medium-sized town situated on a beautiful lake. For decades the inhabitants of this small township of some 25,000 people have lived a fairly isolated life, despite the arrival of television and the fact that national newspapers are on sale. However, a group of local business people has started discussions with an international hotel chain to establish tourism in the area. At the same time, the neighbouring Harulang tribe, who are artistically very active, want to cash in on tourism by offering tours to their forest and village.

The closest large city is two hours away on dirt roads, but the natural beauty of the area seems to offer opportunities to draw tourists from the city and from abroad to this area. The hotel operators wish to tackle the project cautiously and have consulted with people in the town, as well as with elders from surrounding tribes. There is a general feeling of excitement, but also of fear: many people are afraid that the traditional way of life will get lost.

A seminar has been organized to bring representatives of the stakeholders together for a discussion.

Inhabitants	25,000
Closest city	Shanda (100,000 inhabitants)
Closest airport	Haru (only light planes)
Distances	100 km to Shanda
	30 km to coast
	100 m to lake
Road conditions	dirt roads, some tarmac
Indiginous attraction	Harulang tribe (500 people), active art community
Natural attractions	river, lake, rainforest

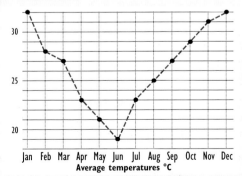

Average temperatures °C

Recognizing fixed phrases from tourism and hospitality (2)

Make sure you understand and can pronounce these phrases and words.

budget travel
destination planning
developing country
health resort
host country
low-income jobs
mainstream tourism
natural resources
public health
retail development
tourist destination

Recognizing fixed phrases from academic English (2)

Make sure you understand these fixed phrases from general spoken academic English.

As we shall see, ...
But the real question is ...
From the point of view of ...
In a case like this ...
In terms of ...
In the sense that ...
In this sort of situation ...
The first thing is ...
That's the reason why ...
Increasingly, we find that ...
It could be argued that ...
It's true to say that ...
Many people think ...
On the grounds that ...
On the one hand, ...
Research has shown that ...
So it should be clear that ...
That would be great, except ...
To some extent ...
To start with, ...

Using the Cornell note-taking system

There are many ways to take notes from a lecture. One method was developed by Walter Pauk at Cornell University, USA.

The system involves **Five Rs**.

record	Take notes during the lecture.
reduce	After the lecture, turn the notes into one- or two-word questions or 'cues' which will help you remember the key information.
recite	Say the questions and answers aloud.
reflect	Decide on the best way to summarize the key information in the lecture.
review	Look again at the key words and the summary (and do this regularly).

Recognizing digressions

Lecturers sometimes move away from the main point in a lecture to tell a story or an anecdote. This is called a **digression**. You must be able to recognize the start and end of digressions in a lecture.

Sometimes a digression is directly relevant to the content of the lecture, sometimes it has some relevance and sometimes, with a poor lecturer, it may be completely irrelevant. Sometimes the lecturer points out the relevance.

Don't worry if you get lost in a digression. Just leave a space in your notes and ask people afterwards.

Recognizing the start	*That reminds me …*
	I remember once …
	By the way …
Recognizing the end	*Anyway, where was I?*
	Back to the point.
	So, as I was saying …

Understanding the relevance	*Of course, the point of that story is …*
	I'm sure you can all see that the story shows …
	Why did I tell that story? Well, …

Asking about digressions	*What was the point of the story about Tibet?*
	Why did she start talking about note-taking?
	I didn't get the bit about …

Referring to other people's ideas

We often need to talk about the ideas of other people in a lecture or a tutorial. We normally give the name of the writer and/or the name of the source. We usually introduce the reference with a phrase; we may quote directly, or we may paraphrase an idea.

Name and introducing phrase	*As Leiper points out …*
	To quote Leiper …
Where	*in* Principles of Tourism *…*
What	*we can think of culture as …*

10.1 Vocabulary
'neutral' and 'marked' words • expressing confidence/tentativeness

A Study the words in box a.

1 Use your dictionary to find out the meanings.

2 What part of speech is each word?

> **a** adopt   commitment   corporate
> empower   enhance   implement
> operational   perform   productivity
> strategic   tactical

B Read the Hadford University handout.

1 Use your dictionary or another source to check the meanings of the highlighted phrases.

2 Which are the stressed syllables in each phrase?

C Look at the pictures on the opposite page.

1 Who are the people in each picture? What kind of organization do they work for?

2 Describe which role in the organization these people fulfil.

3 Indicate where they would be on the organization chart.

D Study the words in box b.

1 Check the meanings, parts of speech and stress patterns.

2 Put the words into the correct box in the table below, as in the example.

Neutral	Marked
rise, increase	rocket, soar
fall, decrease	
big, large	
good	
small	

HADFORD University

Changes in corporate management

In tourism and hospitality there appears to be a shift from companies using process-oriented management, where standardized operating systems are important, to adopting performance-driven management, where empowerment of workers is central. A top-down management style does not always seem to serve business interests best. Therefore, employee involvement has become a business strategy for many operations. However, managers are still important in deciding how to use human resources and how to implement long-term strategic decisions.

> **b** brilliant   collapse   enormous
> fantastic   great   huge   insignificant
> massive   minimal   minor   outstanding
> plummet   rocket   significant   slump
> soar   superb   tremendous

E Read the extract from a chairman's letter to shareholders.

1 Use a marked word in place of each of the blue (neutral) words.

2 Look at the red phrases. How strong or confident are they?

It is generally accepted now that companies need to involve their staff in important decisions. Undoubtedly, the number of departments in our company empowering employees is rising, but it is fair to say that empowerment is not large in this organization at present, and we have a good opportunity to improve in this area. We may start to introduce changes over the next few months. You can be confident, however, that we will not make any managerial changes which lead to a fall in profits.

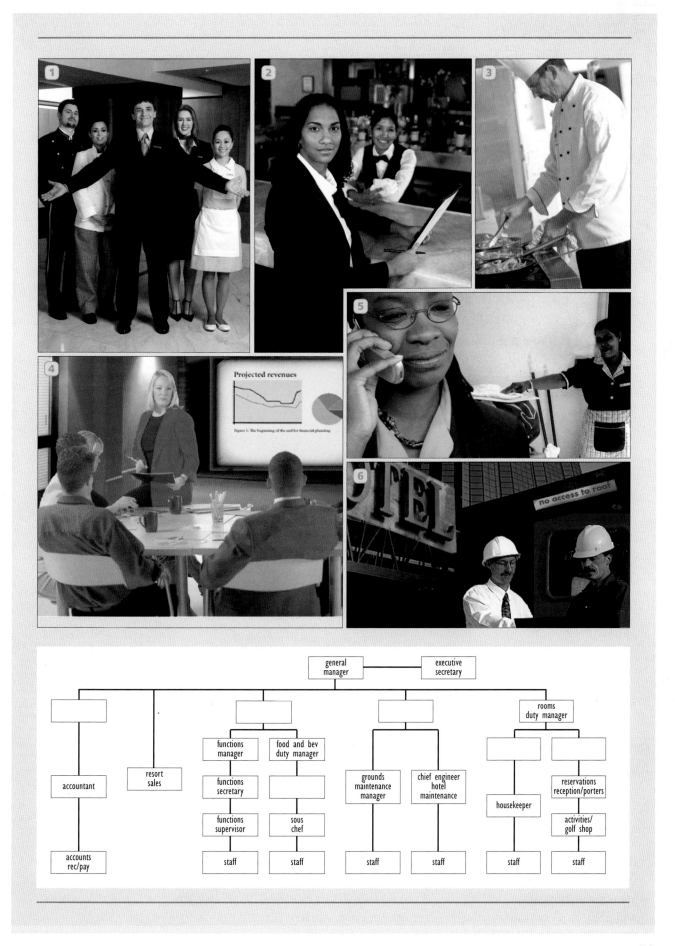

A Study the sentence on the right. Each phrase in box a could go in the space. What effect would each one have on the base meaning? Mark from *** = very confident to * = very tentative.

Poor management last year _____ the decline in visitor numbers.

B Survey the text on the opposite page.
   1 What will the text be about?
   2 Write three research questions.

C Read the text. Does it answer your questions?

D Answer these questions.
   1 What level of decision-making is involved when a company decides to merge with another?
   2 A tour operator decides to try to buy extra rooms for one season only. What kind of aim is this?
   3 What is the opposite of a top-down management style?
   4 What reason does Murphy give for the need for good management?
   5 What does Page believe is the main objective of most tourism producers?
   6 What is Leiper's case study an example of?
   7 Who has to change in Buhalis and Costa's 'transformations'?

a
  probably caused _____
  may have contributed to _____
  was possibly one of the factors which contributed to _____
  could have been a factor which led to _____
  caused _____
  seems to have caused _____

b
  It is obvious ... _____
  Many writers seem to agree ... _____
  It appears to be the case ... _____
  many writers have claimed ... _____
  Leiper's 1995 study found ... _____
  Much of the data in that study suggests ... _____

E Find the phrases in box b in the text. Is the writer *confident* (**C**) or *tentative* (**T**) about the information which follows?

F Study the last sentence of the last paragraph.
   1 Underline the marked words the writer uses.
   2 What does the choice of these words tell you about the writer's opinion of the Hilton chain?
   3 Find neutral words to use in their place.

Example:

Many **writers** | seem to agree | that | in **tourism,** | as in any other **business,** | **management** | takes place | at three **levels**: strategic, tactical and operational.

A

However, many smaller businesses, like the resort described below, opt for a different solution altogether, which Briedenhann and Wickens define as 'empowerment and progressive capacity-building of local people into management positions.'

B

In recent years, many writers have claimed that decentralizing management has a very positive effect on the success of a business, but not all evidence supports that belief.

G Study the example sentence on the right, and then sentences A and B.
   1 Divide sentences A and B into small parts, as in the example sentence.
   2 Underline any linking words (e.g., conjunctions).
   3 Find the subjects, verbs, objects/complements and adverbial phrases which go together.
   4 Make several short simple sentences which show the meaning.

Top-down or bottom-up?

All businesses need good management, and one important principle that managers should follow is 'focus on the customer'. It is obvious, therefore, that 'Organisations that specialise exclusively or largely in tourism need business strategies centred around tourists' (Leiper, 2004, p. 259).

Many writers seem to agree that in tourism, as in any other business, management takes place at three levels: strategic, tactical and operational. *Strategic* decisions are long-term, affect the whole organization and are made by senior managers. They are complex and based on uncertain information. *Tactical* decisions are focused on how to implement strategic decisions. They are medium-term, made by heads of business units, and affect parts of the organization. *Operational* decisions are concerned with short-term aims and day-to-day management. Junior managers or supervisors can make these decisions.

It appears to be the case that, despite sharing general principles, tourism and hospitality organizations structure themselves in many different ways depending on where they are, what size they are and what they offer. Some, especially for instance large hotel chains, will often adopt a traditional top-down style, with a general manager and a management team representing human resources, finance, operations, marketing, IT, legal, etc. However, many smaller businesses, like the resort described below, opt for a different solution altogether, which Briedenhann and Wickens define as 'empowerment and progressive capacity-building of local people into management positions.' (Richards, 2007, p. 88). A large number of companies seem to adopt this management style and many try to combine the two.

Murphy and Murphy (2004) claim that pulling 'the various industry and community components together to form an approved and competitive community tourism product will be fundamental to the success of a destination' (pp. 405–406). They go on to say that this process needs good management in the form of leadership. Page (2006) asserts that the majority of businesses involved 'in the delivery and production of tourism products ... operate for a profit motive, and for them to achieve this objective they need management in order to get things done.' (p. 249)

Leiper (1995) describes how the manager of a Pacific resort changed the way it was run and the roles of the employees. He changed a resort hotel with more than 100 accommodation units into eight small hotels arranged around shared facilities (front desk, pool and restaurants) and allowed the new hotels to be operated without GM supervision or line managers. In doing so, the owner combined two management theories. The first is that 'breaking up big organisations in small teams can enhance productivity and quality' (Leiper, 1995, p. 272). The second states that 'empowering workers, giving them the right to make decisions on matters which might otherwise require managerial authority, can enhance quality and encourage commitment from employees' (ibid.).

In recent years, many writers have claimed that decentralizing management has a very positive effect on the success of a business, but not all evidence supports that belief. For example, Leiper's 1995 study found that the resort experienced considerable managerial difficulty. This was partly caused by managers who could not adapt to a new role which required them to coach rather than manage. Also, workers found it difficult to deal with the new responsibilities. Much of the data in that study suggests that the experience was typical and confirms the suspicion that empowerment is a feature that needs strict management. At the time of writing, the hotel seems to have gone back to its previous centralized management style.

Buhalis and Costa (2005) talk about tourism initiatives that show three characteristics: 'first, a shift away from centralized, process-oriented bureaucracies to more decentralized, performance-driven management structures; secondly, a shift away from fragmented, standardized operating systems to more ... integrated forms of working where there is greater employee involvement and empowerment; thirdly, a change in the role of managers' (p. 87).

However, as Evans, Campbell and Stonehouse (2003) assert, in 'all industries ... some organizations are more successful than others. This is as true for ... travel and tourism as for any other industry. The best performers ... possess something special that weaker competitors do not have and this enables them to outperform their rivals.' (p. 48) After all, even very large companies start small, as can be seen in the case of the Hilton brand. Its development has been astonishing, from an insignificant one-hotel operation in 1919 to a gigantic global brand almost a century later.

A Read the four essay questions. What types of essays are they?

B Look at text A on the opposite page. Copy and complete Table 1 below.

C Look at text B on the opposite page. Copy and complete Table 2.

D Read the title of essay 4 again.

1 Make a plan for this essay.

2 Write a topic sentence for each paragraph in the body of the essay.

3 Write a concluding paragraph.

1 Compare decisions a company might take to achieve a short-term goal, and those it might take to achieve a long-term goal.

2 Explain from a managerial viewpoint how some of a company's main resources might help it to achieve its goals.

3 Outline some of the ways in which a company can raise finance for its operations.

4 Describe, with some examples, the financial problems faced by small tourism or hospitality business start-ups. Consider how small businesses can best solve these difficulties.

Table 1

Situation	
Problem	
Solutions	

Table 2

Solution	
Argument for	
Argument against	

A Expand these simple sentences. Add extra information. Use the ideas you discussed in Lessons 2 and 3.

1 High street banks do not always give loans to new small businesses.

2 Small entrepreneurs cannot issue shares to the public.

3 Not all evidence shows that decentralizing management is positive.

4 Allowing employees to take strategic decisions is risky.

B Look at the reference list (C) on the opposite page. Copy and complete Tables 1–3.

C Look at the pages from a book (D) on the opposite page.

1 Complete a further row of Table 1.

2 How could you write this as a reference?

D What do the abbreviations in the blue box mean?

E Look back at the text on page 81 (Lesson 2).

1 Find all the research sources (e.g., Leiper, 2004, page 259).

2 Add the page numbers to the correct reference in the list on the opposite page.

3 What punctuation is used to introduce each direct quote?

4 What words are used to introduce each direct quote? Why does the writer choose each word?

Table 1: *Referencing books*

Author(s)	Date	Place	Publisher

Table 2: *Referencing journals*

Name of journal	Volume	Pages

Table 3: *Referencing websites*

Retrieval date	URL

| & | © | cf. | edn. | ed(s). | et al. |
| ibid. | n.d. | op. cit. | p. | pp. | vol. |

Ⓐ

Case Study 1: Financing a tourism business

In 2006, Alison Cole left her nine-to-five job and set up a company called Moreton's Myth Horse Treks which organized horse-riding adventures for tourists. She operated from her five-acre country property. Her high street bank refused her a loan but agreed to an overdraft of £4,000. With this and a government Small Business Start-up loan of £5,000, Alison was able to lease a stall in a market in her local town and also set up a website through which she could sell her treks. When, in 2007, she wanted to expand her business to a small stables operating from the local park, her bank again refused her a loan, despite the fact that she was now beginning to make a profit. Eventually, Alison borrowed the money from her mother and brother.

(adapted from Venture, 2005)

Ⓑ

Management of a small hospitality business involves dealing with money as much as with people. It is clear that small businesses cannot rely on banks for financial help. Another alternative which may be considered by small entrepreneurs is to raise finance through the sale of equity in the business to a venture capitalist (Brookes, 2003). Grange (2005) argues that this represents 'a sound option' (p. 34) since these investors are often experienced business people and the small business owner may benefit from their business advice. However, Grange (ibid.) also points out that, 'The disadvantage is that the small entrepreneur is no longer the sole owner, and more importantly perhaps, may well see their hard-earned profits go to someone else.'

Ⓒ

References

Briedenhann, J., & Wickens, E. (2007). Developing cultural tourism in South Africa: potential and pitfalls. In Richards, G. (Ed.) *Cultural tourism: Global and local perspectives*. Binghamton, NY: The Haworth Press.

Buhalis, D., & Costa, C. (Eds.). (2005). *Tourism management dynamics: Trends, management and tools*. Oxford: Elsevier/Butterworth-Heinemann.

Evans, N., Campbell, D., & Stonehouse, S. (2003). *Strategic management for travel and tourism*. Oxford: Elsevier/Butterworth-Heinemann.

Hilton Hotels. (n.d.). *Hilton hotels*. Retrieved January 12, 2007, from http://en.wikipedia.org/wiki/Hilton_Hotels

Leiper, N. (1995). *Tourism management*. Melbourne: RMIT Publishing.

Leiper, N. (2004). *Tourism management* (3rd ed.). Frenchs Forest, NSW: Pearson Education Australia.

Murphy, P., & Murphy, A. (2004). *Strategic management for tourism communities: Bridging the gaps*. Clevedon: Channel View Publications.

Northcote, J., & Macbeth, J. (2006). Conceptualizing yield: Sustainable tourism management. *Annals of Tourism Research*, *33*(1), 199–220.

Page, S. (2006). *Tourism management: Managing for change* (2nd ed.). Oxford: Elsevier/Butterworth-Heinemann.

Ⓓ

Case Studies in Tourism and Hospitality Businesses

Miriam Whitmarsh

Wentworth & Bourne

First published in 2006
by Wentworth & Bourne Ltd.
11 Vine Lane, London EC4P 5EI
© 2006 Miriam Whitmarsh
Reprinted 2007

British Library Cataloguing-in-Publication Data
A catalogue record for this book is available from the British Library

Typeset by Glenda Graphics, Barnstaple, Devon, UK
Printed and bound by PW Enterprises, Bude, Cornwall, UK
ISBN 0-321-09487-4

Recognizing fixed phrases from tourism and hospitality studies (3)

Make sure you understand these key phrases relating to management.

top-down management style	*business strategy*	*human resources*
process-oriented management style	*business interests*	*management team*
strategic decision	*long-term*	*senior manager*
tactical decision	*medium-term*	*line manager*
operational decision	*short-term*	*employee involvement*

Recognizing fixed phrases from academic English (3)

Make sure you understand these key phrases from general academic English.

One of the …	*In this sort of situation …*
In some circumstances, …	*It is obvious/clear that …*
Even so, …	*It appears to be the case that …*
… , as follows: …	*Research has shown …*
The writers conclude/assume/suggest that …	*The evidence does not support this idea.*

Recognizing levels of confidence in research or information

In an academic context, writers will usually indicate the level of confidence in information they are giving. When you read a 'fact' in a text, look for qualifying words before it, which show the level of confidence.

Examples:
It appears to be the case that … / This suggests that … (**tentative**)
The evidence shows that … / It is clear that … (**definite/confident**)

Recognizing 'marked' words

Many common words in English are 'neutral', i.e., they do not imply any view on the part of the writer or speaker. However, there are often apparent synonyms which are 'marked'. They show attitude, or stance.

Example:

Neutral	Marked
*Occupancy rates **rose** by 10% last year.*	*Occupancy rates **soared** by 10% last year.*

When you read a sentence, think: *Is this a neutral word, or is it a marked word? If it is marked, what does this tell me about the writer's attitude to the information?*

When you write a sentence, think: *Have I used neutral words or marked words? If I have used marked words, do they show my real attitude/the attitude of the original writer?*

Extend your vocabulary by learning marked words and their exact effect.

Examples:

Neutral	Marked
go down, fall, decrease	*slump, plummet*
say, state	*assert, maintain, claim, argue, allege*
good	*great, brilliant, tremendous*

Identifying the parts of a long sentence

Long sentences contain many separate parts. You must be able to recognize these parts to understand the sentence as a whole. Mark up a long sentence as follows:

- Locate the subjects, verbs and objects/complements and underline the relevant words.
- Put a dividing line:
  - at the end of a phrase which begins a sentence
  - before a phrase at the end of the sentence
  - between clauses
- Put brackets round extra pieces of information.

Example:

In recent years many writers have claimed that decentralizing management has a very positive effect on the success of a business, but some evidence does not support that belief.

In recent years | many <u>writers</u> have <u>claimed</u> | that <u>decentralizing management</u> has a very positive <u>effect</u> (on the success of a business,) | but some <u>evidence</u> <u>does not support</u> that <u>belief</u>.

Constructing a long sentence

Begin with a very simple SV(O)(C)(A) sentence and then add extra information.

Example:

	Small companies		**need**	**help.**		
As many recent studies have shown,	*small companies*	*in every kind of industry*	*need*	*help*	*of many kinds,*	*including money and advice.*

Writing a bibliography/reference list

The APA (American Psychological Association) system is probably the most common in the social sciences. Information should be given as shown in the following source references for a book, an Internet article and a journal article. The final list should be in alphabetical order according to the family name of the writer. See the reference list on page 83 for a model.

Author	Date	Title of book	Place of publication	Publisher
Leiper, N.	(1995).	*Tourism management.*	Melbourne:	RMIT Publishing.

Writer or organization	Date (or 'n.d.')	Title of Internet article	Date of retrieval	Full URL
Google.	(2007).	*Hilton hotels.*	Retrieved December 4, 2007, from	http://en.wikipedia.org/wiki/Hilton_Hotels

Author	Date	Title of article	Title of journal	Volume and page numbers
Northcote, J., & Macbeth, J.	(2006).	Conceptualizing yield: Sustainable tourism management.	*Annals of Tourism Research.*	*33,* 199–220.

More information on referencing (including other systems such as MLA) can be found on: http://owl.english.purdue.edu/owl/resource/560/05/ or www.westwords.com/guffey/apa.html

11 EXTERNAL INFLUENCES

11.1 Vocabulary   linking ideas

A Look at the diagram on the opposite page.

1 Name the five factors.

2 Discuss how the examples of each factor might influence businesses.

3 Give more examples of each factor.

B Study the linking words and phrases in box a.

1 Put them into two groups for:
   a discussing reasons and results
   b building an argument.

2 Is each linking word used to join ideas:
   a within a sentence?
   b between sentences?

3 Can you think of similar linking words?

4 Put the linking words in question 1 b in a suitable order to list points in support of an argument.

C Study the words in box b.

1 Sort the words into groups according to whether they are mainly concerned with *people* or with *change* or both.

2 In pairs, explain your decisions.

3 Are the words nouns, verbs or adjectives? What is their stress pattern?

4 What other words or phrases have the same meaning?

D Read the text on the right.

1 Complete each space with a word or phrase from box a or box b. Change the form if necessary.

2 Can you think of other words or phrases with the same meaning as the blue words?

3 Highlight all the words and phrases in the text connected with *people and work* or *change*.

4 Match the phrases below with a later phrase in the text that refers back to them, as in the example.

   Example:
   people ... in their 70s – these elderly employees

   the effects   fewer young people
   parts of the world   markets

E Do the quiz on the opposite page.

---

a
Another point is ...   As a result,
because   Finally,   Firstly,   For example,
In addition,   Moreover,
One result of this is ...   Secondly,   since   So,

b
affect   ageing   consultant   diversify
effect   elderly   immigrant   part-timer
population   rethink   shrink   youth

According to Peter Drucker (2001), a well-known business thinker, there are many demographic changes which will _____ businesses profoundly over the next 25 years. Firstly, the _____ is ageing and _____ patterns of employment will _____ . For _____ , provision of pensions for retired people is becoming an increasingly serious problem for governments. _____ many people will have to continue in their jobs until they are in their 70s. In _____ , these _____ employees are not likely to work for companies on a full-time basis but as _____ , part-timers or temporary staff.

_____ , there are the effects of fewer young people in many parts of the world. _____ that many of these countries will have to rely more and more on an _____ labour force.

_____ that markets will need to change: because the falling numbers of younger people mean fewer families, businesses which have built their markets on the basis of the family unit will now have to _____ their approach.

_____ , up to now there has been an emphasis on the _____ market; from now on, the middle-aged segment is likely to dominate. _____ , since the supply of younger workers will _____ , businesses will have to find new ways to attract and retain staff.

Source: Drucker, P. (2001, November 3–9). The next society. *The Economist*, pp. 3–20.

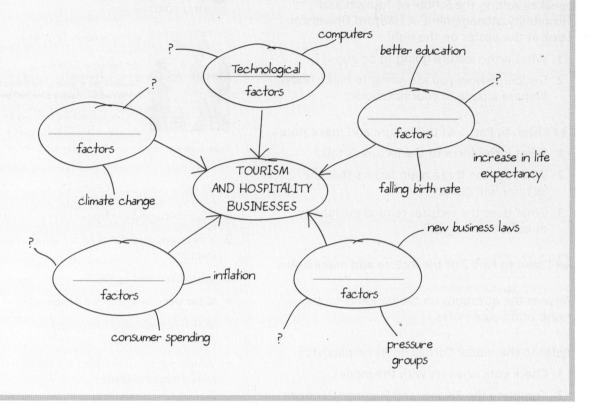

What factors have an impact on tourism and hospitality businesses?

Technological factors
? computers

? factors
better education
? factors
increase in life expectancy
falling birth rate

? factors
climate change

TOURISM AND HOSPITALITY BUSINESSES

? factors
inflation
consumer spending

? factors
new business laws
pressure groups

HADFORD *University*

Sustainable tourism quiz

What makes tourism, and you, responsible?

1 How would *you* define tourism?

2 Tourism is most popular in coastal areas. Give examples of coastal tourism.

3 Tourism is not considered an environmentally friendly industry. Why not?

4 Which one of these is NOT a key aim of sustainable tourism?

   a   social responsibility

   b   profit for tour operators

   c   commitment to conservation

   d   integration of local people

5 Which organizations should be involved in making tourism sustainable?

6 Tourism operators should have an environmental audit. What is the purpose of this?

7 What do you think the Golden Rules of sustainable tourism are for *tourists*? Complete these sentences:

   a   Think of your holiday as …

   b   Have respect for …

   c   Don't waste …

   d   Leave nothing behind but footprints – take nothing away but …

   e   Use non-polluting forms of …

   f   Keep a sense of humour when …

   g   Choose your holiday …

A You are going to listen to a lecture by a guest speaker visiting the School of Tourism and Hospitality Management at Hadford University. Look at the poster on the right.

   1 What is the lecture going to be about?

   2 Decide on how you are going to make notes. Prepare a page in your notebook.

B 🎧 Listen to Part 1 of the lecture and make notes.

   1 What is the focus of the lecturer's talk?

   2 What are the three main factors that the lecturer will discuss?

   3 What does the lecturer remind everybody of before he begins?

C 🎧 Listen to Part 2 of the lecture and make notes.

D Answer the questions on the handout on the right, using your notes.

E Refer to the model Cornell notes on page 106.

   1 Check your answers with the model.

   2 Complete the *Review* and *Summary* sections of the Cornell notes.

F 🎧 The lecturer talks about mass tour operators as a case in point. Listen again to that part of the lecture. Which words tell us whether the information is fact or opinion?

G 🎧 Study the phrases in the blue box. Which type of information below follows each phrase? Listen to some sentences from the lecture.

- restatement
- definite point
- summary of a source
- example
- statement of a topic
- another point
- tentative point
- clarification
- purpose for speaking

H Write out one section of your notes in complete sentences.

See Skills bank

HADFORD *University*

Visiting Speaker: Dr William Grayson
15th February 5.00 p.m.
'Tourism as a global business: sustainable checks and balances'

Dr Grayson will explore key factors affecting business decisions in today's global tourism and hospitality environment.

---

1 What factor did the lecturer discuss first?

2 What examples of this factor did the lecturer mention?

3 What happened in 1979?

4 What were the effects for business?

5 Which organization campaigns on environmental issues?

6 Which organization found it hard to recover from a negative image?

7 What does Iceland's whaling industry have to do with the influence of pressure groups?

8 Why could it be hard for tourism organizations to practise sustainable tourism?

9 What type of economic activity has decreased and what type has increased in developed countries?

10 What might be the effects of the increasing economic power of countries such as India and China?

---

1 that is to say ...

2 Don't misunderstand me.

3 To some degree, ...

4 It is fair to say that ...

5 Not only that, but ...

6 In an attempt to ...

7 with respect to ...

8 ... is a case in point.

9 ... gives a good description of ... in ...

10 Briefly, (he) explains how ...

11 (She) has no doubt that ...

11.3 Extending skills
stress in phrases • building an argument

A Study the phrases in box a.

1 Mark the stressed syllables in each phrase.

2  Listen and check your answers.

3 Which phrases have adjective + noun? Which word has the stronger stress in these phrases?

B Look at the topics below.

global warming   pollution   waste management

1 What would you like to know about these topics in relation to tourism and hospitality?

2 Prepare a page in your notebook to make some notes.

3 Listen to the final part of the lecture (Part 3) and make notes. If there is information which you miss, leave a space.

4 Compare your notes with someone else. Fill in any blank spaces.

C Answer the questions on the Hadford University handout, using your notes.

D Study the stages of building an argument (a–f) in box b.

1 Put the stages in an appropriate order.

2 Match each stage (a–f) with a phrase from box c.

E Look at box b again.

1 Listen to a section from the lecture. Make notes of what the lecturer says for each stage of the argument (a–f).

2 Check your answers to Exercises D and E1.

F Use your notes to write 75–100 words about the main points in the final part of the lecture.

G In groups, discuss the research task set by the lecturer. Talk about these questions:

1 What are the three environmental topics you need to consider?

2 Which one will you choose?

3 What ideas do you already have?

4 What kind of information will you need to find?

5 Where can you go to find more information?

Report back to the class on your discussion. In Lesson 4 you will take part in a seminar on this topic.

a
global warming
waste disposal
natural phenomena
business opportunities
threats to the environment
industrial emissions
environmental issues
a positive correlation
aspects such as pollution

HADFORD *University*

1 What seems to be the most serious environmental issue, according to the lecturer?

2 What aspect of the environmental impact of tourism is often forgotten?

3 Who should play a key role in addressing the problem of global warming?

4 What other environmental problems are mentioned in the lecture?

5 What does taking responsibility for these issues mean for business? What is already happening?

6 What is your research task?

b
a giving a counter argument
b giving your opinion
c stating the issue
d supporting the reason with evidence
e rejecting a counter argument
f giving a reason for your opinion

c
It's quite clear that ...
The question is ...
The research has concluded that ...
I'm afraid that just isn't true.
Some people claim ...
The evidence lies in the fact that ...

A Study the terms in box a.

1 Explain the meaning of the terms.

2 Mark the main stress in each term.

B Study the words in box b. Match the words in columns 1 and 2 to make phrases.

C Study the GREENSCAPE.com web page on the opposite page.

1 What three types of energy source are shown in the photos?

2 What opportunities, useful suggestions or threats can you identify for tourism and hospitality businesses? Make three lists.

D Study the phrases in box c.

1 What purpose would you use these phrases for in a seminar?

2 Which phrases can you use for linking your new point to a contribution by another speaker?

E 🎧 Listen to some students taking part in a seminar. They have been asked to discuss new technologies and some of the new environmental initiatives in tourism. While you listen, make a note of:

1 the main topic of each extract

2 further details of each topic

F Study the Waste in the Workplace web page and discuss these questions.

1 What is the main message?

2 What can businesses do to evaluate their level of waste?

3 Look at the 'What a waste!' list. What could tourism and hospitality businesses do about each of the things on the list?

4 What do you think it means to be 'eco-certified', and how could this help tourism and hospitality businesses?

5 What kind of information would you expect to find under the 'Case study' link?

G In groups, discuss your research findings on the positive and negative aspects of environmental initiatives for tourism and hospitality businesses.

One person from the group should report the conclusions of the discussion to the class.

---

a

carbon trading scheme
climate change tax
packaging reduction target
recycling business opportunity
renewable energy source
sustainable accommodation design
transit route pollution
waste disposal regulation

---

b

1	2
biodegradable	energy
carbon	farm
emission	footprint
environmentally	fuel
fossil	impact
greenhouse	packaging
low	gas
nature	friendly
solar	reduction
wave	reserve
wind	power

---

c

I'd like to start by explaining …

To carry on from this first point, I want secondly to look at …

I don't think that is the main reason.

That seems like a very good point X is making.

I'm going to expand the topic by mentioning …

On the other hand, you might want to say that …

As well as this issue, we can also look at a very different issue.

So to sum up, we can say that …

Does anybody have any opinions or anything they would like to add?

I think we need a different viewpoint.

OK, to continue then …

Following on from what X has said …

A

GREENSCAPE.com your tourism and hospitality environmental advisor

| corporate | housing | transport | community | business | projects | home |

Look here for the latest regulations and information on:

Air pollution
- Climate change taxes on businesses
- Join a carbon trading scheme
- Latest international climate change agreements
- Pollution prevention
- Laws on hazardous substances and emissions
- Start your own carbon offset business

Building
- Sustainable building
- How to improve the efficiency of existing facilities

Waste management
- Waste disposal regulations
- Government packaging reduction targets
- Waste in the workplace

Renewable energy
- Install an alternative energy source, save money and help the environment!

Recycling
- Why should we recycle?
- How to recycle your waste
- Look here for recycling opportunities for you and your guests

---

B

Waste in the Workplace

All businesses produce waste as part of their working practices – but this waste is actually a business cost. If a business is as efficient as it possibly can be, there is less waste and therefore lower costs – not only that but you can help the environment too!

What a waste! How to manage your guests ... and yourself.

glass

cooking oil

paper

water

wasted energy

packaging

Get your business eco-certified! Click **here**.

Case study – find out what you can do

Fleet Park

Fleet Park is a family-run holiday park with 25 static hire caravans.

Find out more ...

Tourism businesses need to take a look at how they can reduce waste. For a waste audit and advice on waste reduction, go to http://www.wasteintheworkplace.com./advice

Tip of the week
Ask your guests to change linen every other day: it saves water!

Linking words

We use linking words and phrases to join ideas together in a sequence, to show how the ideas are related.

Some linking words can be used to join independent and dependent clauses in a sentence.

Examples:

*Businesses which have built their markets on the basis of the family unit will now have to rethink their approach, **because** falling numbers of young people mean fewer families.*

OR

__Because__ falling numbers of young people mean fewer families, businesses which have built their markets on the basis of the family unit will now have to rethink their approach.

Other linking words and phrases join sentences in a text.

Example:

*Firstly, the population is ageing. **As a result**, certain types of holiday are likely to become popular.*

When building an argument, it is a good idea to use linking words to add points.

Firstly, …	*Another point is …*	*In addition, …*	*… whereas …*
For example, …	*Secondly, …*	*Moreover, …*	*Finally, …*

Using words with similar meanings to refer back in a text

It is a good idea to learn several words with similar or related meanings. We often build cohesion in a text by using different words to refer back to something previously mentioned.

Examples:

First mention	Second mention	Third mention	Fourth mention
older workers	*elderly employees*	*those of pensionable age*	*people in their 70s*
fewer …	*falling numbers of …*	*declining …*	*reduced …*
parts of the world	*countries*	*areas*	*destinations*

Recognizing fixed phrases from academic English (3)

In Units 7 and 9, we learnt some key fixed phrases from general academic English. Here are some more to use when speaking.

Don't misunderstand me.
I'm afraid that just isn't true.
in an attempt to …
… is a case in point
not only that, but …
Some people say …
the effect of …

the history of …
the presence of …
there is a correlation between … and …
to some degree …
to the extent that …
What's more …
with respect to …

Writing out notes in full

When making notes we use as few words as possible. This means that when we come to write up the notes, we need to pay attention to:

* the use of numbers and symbols for words and ideas, e.g.,
  (1) growth of air travel hard to stop ∴ bottom line = profit for airlines
  The first point is that the growth of air travel is going to be hard to stop, **because** the bottom line **is** profit for the airlines.

* making sure the grammatical words are put back in, e.g.,
  ⟶ many tourists increasingly concerned about impact on environment
  Many tourists **are** increasingly concerned about **their** impact on **the** environment.

* making the implied meanings clear, e.g.,
  political factors (e.g., taxation policies, pressure groups)
  Political factors **which affect tourism include**, for example, taxation policies, pressure groups …

Building an argument

A common way to build an argument is:

1 First, state the issue:
  Can we change people's perception that waste is inevitable?

2 Next, give a counter argument:
  Research has shown that changing attitudes is extremely difficult.

3 Then give your opinion:
  In fact, minimizing waste is far from being a new idea.

4 Then give evidence for your opinion:
  The efficiencies in this holiday farm's waste management approach are based on recycling.

Linking to a previous point

When you want to move the discussion in a new direction, introduce your comments with phrases such as:
Following on from what X said, I'd like to talk about …
I'm going to expand the topic by mentioning …
As well as (carbon offsetting), we can also look at a very different sort of issue.

Summarizing a source

When we talk about the ideas of other people in a lecture or a seminar, we often give a summary of the source in a sentence or two.

Examples:
A book by (name of writer) called (name of book) published in (year) gives an explanation of how …
Briefly, (name of writer) explains how …
An introduction to (topic) can be found in (name of writer).

12 INFORMATION, STRATEGY AND CHANGE

A Study the words and phrases in box a.

  1 How does each word relate to IT in a tourism operation?

  2 Check the stress and pronunciation.

> **a**   Intranet   Extranet   Internet
> management information system
> decision support system
> touch-screen terminal   blog

B Study the words in box b.

  1 How can these people use IT to create better business links with each other?

  2 Discuss your experience of booking online tourism or hospitality.

> **b**   travel agent   tour operator
> retailer   events organizer
> hotelier   restaurant owner
> transport provider   web publisher

C Read text A on the opposite page.

  1 What is a SWOT analysis?

  2 Connect each highlighted item to its noun.
  Example: *it* refers to previously mentioned noun (*company*)

> **c**   accept   agree   argue   assert
> cite   claim   concede   consider
> contend   describe   disagree   dispute
> emphasize   illustrate   indicate
> insist   note   observe   point out
> report   show   state   suggest

D Study the verbs in box c. They can be used to introduce quotations, paraphrases and summaries.

  1 Check the meanings of any words you don't know.

  2 Which verbs have similar meanings?

  3 Which verbs are **not** followed by *that*?

  4 When can you use each verb?

  Example: *accept* = agree but with some reluctance; the idea is often followed by *but*

E Read text B on the opposite page. Look at the highlighted sentences.

Gaia is a boutique holiday resort offering relaxation and personal care to its customers.

  1 What is the function of each sentence?

  Example: *Employees should be involved in workplace decisions* = opinion or recommendation

  2 In an assignment, should you refer directly to the highlighted sentences by **quoting directly** or **paraphrasing**?

  3 Write each sentence with an appropriate introductory verb, a direct quotation or paraphrase, and the source references.

F Look at the SWOT analysis of Gaia Boutique Resort Hotel on the opposite page.
Which functional area (HR, marketing, finance, operations or IT) does each point in the audit refer to?

G How should Gaia respond to the issues affecting its business?

  1 Discuss in pairs.

  2 Write a paragraph giving your recommendations. Include one of your sentences from Exercise E, question 3.

A SWOT analysis

When a company's performance is looking poor, it may need to make some changes. However, before the company can do this, it should establish where it is now through a strategic analysis. A commonly used technique for this is the SWOT analysis. In this method, managers carry out an 'external audit' in which they examine their business and economic environment as well as the market conditions they face in order to understand the opportunities and threats to the company. Secondly, the organization needs to complete an 'internal audit' in which its strengths and weaknesses are compared with those of the competitors. This means that managers should look at all the functional areas: finance, HR, marketing and operations. The results of such audits are presented in a four-box summary of the business's current strengths and weaknesses, and the opportunities and threats which will affect its future development.

From Jones, M. (2007). *Analysing business performance.* Hadford: Hadford University Press.

B Managing change

[1]When a company is planning to make major changes, employees often react in negative ways. So managers need to persuade employees that change is necessary. An important point here is that [2]employees should be involved in workplace decisions. A useful approach is to get all employees to examine their operational practices using a common framework. Clearly, [3]managers must place value on the contributions of staff at all levels, from the boardroom to the shopfloor. [4]As Albert Humphrey, who developed the SWOT analysis technique in the 1960s, asserts, managers must ' … stop thinking that the company is composed of individuals with individual job descriptions and a layer-on-layer authority structure' (Humphrey & Groves, 2003)*. Only when comments and suggestions have been received from everyone, can the company start to consider its objectives and strategies for the future.

* Humphrey, A. & Groves, P. (2003). Turning a downturn into a major upturn. *Finance Today*, 7, 124–126.

From Pickwell, M. (2006). *Introduction to business strategy.* Hadford: Hadford University Press. p. 24.

Gaia SWOT analysis

Internal audit	Strengths	Weaknesses
	• Staff are experienced and skilled at making visitors feel at home. • Advertising costs have not been high because most advertising is done via the Internet. • Accommodation and services are high quality and modern. • The resort is well placed in an area of natural beauty close to town.	• A lot of money is tied up in real estate. • Sales figures are beginning to dip. • Profits are down on the same period last year. We could make a loss this year. • Some staff are absent a lot – through poor motivation. • The resort is badly presented on its website and there are no links with third parties. • Wages are increasing. • Management information is not readily available.
External audit	Opportunities	Threats
	• Increased leisure time and good pension schemes allow 'baby boomers' to spend more money. • A new tour operator with a global network has recently been in touch to discuss cooperation. • The Internet is now a growing source of information and a tool for booking. • There will be a new land release next to the resort.	• A new tourism developer has shown interest in the new land release and wants to build a luxury resort with all facilities. • Local business taxes will increase next year. • The national tourism board has been focusing attention on adventure holidays, because they want to target a younger generation.

A Discuss the following questions.

  1 What do customers expect from an online tourism service?

  2 How can tourism and hospitality operations use IT to ensure that they are successful?

B Survey the text on the opposite page. What will the text be about? Write three questions to which you would like answers.

C Read the text. Does it answer your questions?

D Number the sentences on the right 1–9 to show the order in which the information is presented in the text.

E For each paragraph:

  1 Identify the topic sentence.

  2 Think of a suitable title.

F Look at the underlined words in the text. What do they refer back to?

G Study the highlighted words in the text.

  1 What linking words and phrases can you use to show:
  • contrast?
  • concession?
  • result?
  • reason?

  2 Write the sentences again, using other linking words or phrases with similar meanings.

H Read the text on the right. A student has written about part of Hitchins' article, but the quotations and paraphrases have not been correctly done. Can you spot the mistakes and correct them?

I Write a paragraph for a university lecturer, summarizing the development of the *tourism distribution channel* as described in paragraph 3 of Hitchins' article. Decide whether you should quote or paraphrase the material from the text.

	Virtual tourism may be good for the environment.
	IT is defined as the tools that enable management.
	IT systems support back- and front-of-house systems.
	Tourism organizations now rely on the complex integration of technological systems.
	Business activities can be divided into primary and support processes.
	Some operators in tourism and hospitality need to redefine their roles.
	The tourism and hospitality distribution channel has become complicated.
	IT systems offer tourism operators many advantages.
	Virtual tourism is growing fast.

As Hitchins (2007) explains that successfully integrating technology … makes it easier to run a tourism business. Many organizations of all sizes now integrate the Internet with Intranet and Extranet to communicate with customers, business partners and employees.

According to Hitchins, he says that almost all travel sites now enable customers to plan their holiday from A to Z and demonstrating that integration of information technology tools is paramount to travel organizations.

HOTEL *monthly*

A great experience

By Michael Hitchins

Technological progress has revolutionized the way we think, act and even travel. Buhalis (2003) writes: 'Tourism and technology go hand in hand' (p. 2). Kamel (2003) agrees: 'Tourism is among the largest online industries and is one of the most important kinds of commerce through the Web' (p. 246). In tourism and hospitality, we define IT as the technological tools that enable strategic, tactical and operational management. It allows operators to manage information and processes, take decisions, communicate directly with customers and sell their products. Consequently, IT has become, with other core functions, such as marketing, finance, HR and operations, a major asset for any company in tourism or hospitality. It cannot be left out of the SWOT analysis.

Successfully integrating technology across an operation makes it easier to run a tourism business. Organizations, big and small, now often depend on the complex interaction of Internet (for communication between a company and its customers), Intranet (for communication between employees and departments *within* a company) and Extranet (for communication between different parts of large global companies or between a company and its immediate suppliers). But despite the fact that IT systems have become more and more complex, travelling has never been easier. Go to any travel site these days and you will be offered the opportunity to book hotels, flights, cars, catering and entertainment, and create exactly the experience you want, demonstrating that integration of information technology tools is paramount to travel organizations.

IT can play a role in all business activities, both *primary* or *support*. In tourism, most of the *primary* activities are called 'front of house' because they are visible to the consumer (for instance, advertising, reservations, check-in and payments). Most *support* activities are called 'back of house' (for instance, accounting, pricing and marketing). IT applications exist for all these activities. For front-of-house activities, there are such things as computer reservation systems, touch-screen terminals that allow you to check in, Internet-based travel intermediaries (such as Expedia), or interactive websites and blogs where customers compare notes. For back-of-house activities, there are management information systems (MIS), decision support systems (DSS) and strategic information systems (SIS). Although all these applications are interconnected and seem to work well, the tourism distribution channel has become a complex system involving travel agents, tour operators, retailers, managers of attractions, providers of accommodation and catering, and many more players, as Figure 1 shows.

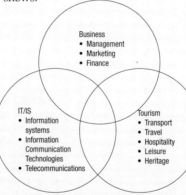

Fig.1. from: Buhalis, D. (2003). *eTourism: Information technology for stategic tourism management*, p. 77

There are many advantages of integrated systems for a tourism operator. They can offer information on destinations, events and attractions, facilitate interaction, establish clubs for customers, provide special offers and deals, and create additional services through partnerships with other companies. In short, they add value to the industry and that is what it is all about. However, there are also some disadvantages in the explosive growth of IT in the tourism and hospitality industry. One is the fact that some parties in the value chain seem to have become unnecessary. Tour operators and travel agencies, for example, primarily act as booking offices. As a result it looks as if they are not adding much value. As travellers become more informed and more independent – especially young, experienced and educated travellers – they want to decide for themselves where to go, how to get there and what to do. Tour operators and agencies will need to re-establish their position and realize that they are service providers who possess knowledge and information their customers want. Perhaps this should be seen as an opportunity. Their niche could be the human touch in what many travellers are coming to see as an impersonal industry.

Tourism operates in an environment undergoing a great transformation, and new technological developments, such as virtual tourism, are growing fast. Virtual-reality museums, virtual communities, personalized electronic travel guides and mobile mapping software are all enabling us to experience tourism destinations before we even go there. Not to mention the virtual communities like Second Life, where virtual tour operators are guiding tours in online worlds and offering virtual holidays, and where real-life travel agents are setting up office. Is this perhaps the ultimate answer to the environmental constraints on global tourism? ■

References

Buhalis, D. (2003). *eTourism: Information technology for strategic tourism management*. Harlow: Pearson Education.

Kamel, S. (2003). *Managing globally with information technology*. Hershey: IGI Global.

6

A Study the words in box a.

  1 Check the pronunciation and grammar.

  2 What are their meanings in a research report?

B Read the introduction to Report A and the conclusion to Report B on the opposite page.

  1 What methods were used in each piece of research?

  2 What are the elements of an introduction and a conclusion?

C Read the two *Method* paragraphs on the right.

  1 Put the verbs in brackets in the correct form.

  2 Identify the original research questions, the research methods and other important information.

D What are the sections of a research report? What order should they go in?

a

conduct data discussion findings
implication interview interviewee
interviewer limitation method
questionnaire random recommendation
research question respondent results
sample survey undertake

Report A: Method

A written questionnaire *(design)* to find out perceptions of Gaia's quality of service and how Gaia *(see)* in relation to its competitors. Two thousand questionnaires *(send)* to a random sample of Gaia's customers, of which 150 *(return)*. In addition, 130 people *(interview)* while spending time at the resort during one day in June. Seventy per cent of the whole sample *(be)* people over 50.

Report B: Method

In order to find out the business activities of some successful boutique hotel companies, a survey of their websites *(undertake)* during the first week of June. The companies which *(investigate)* were Hideaway, Paradise and Just4You.

A Describe the data in Figures 1 and 2 on the opposite page.

B Look at the first paragraph from the *Findings* section of Report A on the right.

  1 Complete the paragraph with linking words and quantity phrases. Put the verbs in the correct tense.

  2 Write another paragraph, using Figures 1 and 2.

C Look at the Internet research notes on the opposite page.

  1 Match the business strategies in box b with an *activity* and a *reason* for doing it from the research notes.

  2 Read the *Findings* section from Report B on page 104. Write a discussion paragraph for Report B using ideas from the notes.

Report A: Findings

_____ , on the negative side, _____ (79%) of customers *(say)* that Gaia's range of services was not varied enough. Only _____ (10%) *(rate)* them as good quality. _____ , a _____ minority (45%) of repeat customers *(state)* that the quality of services over the past five years *(deteriorate)*. _____ , _____ the respondents (71%) *(want)* Gaia to provide more virtual services.

b

building a community
diversification
developing management information systems
joint venture/cooperation

Report A: Introduction

For a long time, Gaia Boutique Resort Hotel has been a highly successful business. However, because the company has lost market share recently, it is important to know what the customers think of the services provided. This report will describe a survey undertaken to find out customers' attitudes towards Gaia Boutique Resort Hotel. Recommendations will also be made as to how the company can improve its customer care.

Report B: Conclusion

To conclude, it is clear that resort businesses which have prospered and grown are now making use of a wide range of IT technology, including the opportunity for customers to have a virtual tourism experience. In addition, in order to maintain success, a company needs to have strong financial control and to consider strategies such as joint ventures with tour operators, travel agents, local retailers and important tourist attractions. In our opinion, Gaia Boutique Resort Hotel should consider such strategies and look closely at the methods adopted by its competitors. Unless action is taken urgently, the company is in danger of going out of business. There is no reason why the company should not have a bright future if the right decisions are taken.

Report A

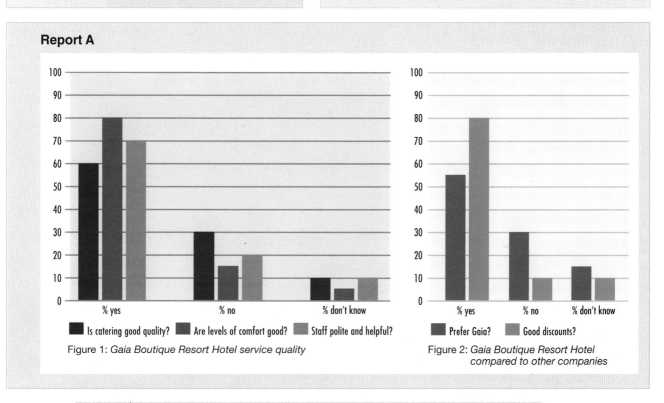

Figure 1: *Gaia Boutique Resort Hotel service quality*

Figure 2: *Gaia Boutique Resort Hotel compared to other companies*

Report B	
Internet research notes on searches of boutique hotel companies	
Activity	Reason/result?
1 invest in IT infrastructure	A create wider customer base
2 cooperate with providers abroad	B ability to take stategic decisions
(travel agents, tour operators)	C customer loyalty, return visits
3 establish clubs for customers	D greater access to new services
4 offer new types of activities	

Introductory verbs

Choosing the right introductory verb is important. Your choice of introductory verb shows what kind of statement the writer is making.

Example:

Pickwell (2006) argues that everyone should be involved in shaping a company's future.

Your choice of introductory verb also shows what you think of another writer's ideas. This is an important part of academic work.

Example:

Hitchins (2007) claims that Gaia failed to take adequate account of IT factors.

Verb	The writer ...
agree	thinks this idea from someone else is true
accept, concede	reluctantly thinks this idea from someone else is true
consider, emphasize, note, observe, point out, state, suggest*	is giving his/her opinion
argue, assert, claim, contend, insist	is giving an opinion that others may not agree with
cite	is referring to someone else's ideas
disagree, dispute	thinks an idea is wrong
suggest*	is giving his/her recommendation
describe	is giving a definition/description
illustrate, indicate, show	is explaining, possibly with an example
report	is giving research findings

*suggest can have two meanings

Linking ideas in a text

Linking words, which join ideas within a sentence or between sentences, convey different meanings.

	Within sentences	Between sentences
Contrast	*but, whereas, while*	*However, In/By contrast, On the other hand*
Concession	*although, despite/ in spite of the fact that*	*However, At the same time, Nevertheless, Despite/In spite of + noun, Yet*
Result	*so, so that*	*So, As a result, Consequently, Therefore*
Reason	*because, since, as*	*Because of + noun, Owing to + noun, Due to + noun*

Referring to quantities and group sizes in a report

A/An	*overwhelming/large/significant slight/small/insignificant/tiny*	*majority*	*(of + noun)*
		minority	
		number	
Over		*half*	
More	*than*	*a quarter a third*	
Less		*x %*	

Structuring a research report

A research report is an account of some research which has been undertaken to find out about a situation or a phenomenon, e.g., *What do our customers think of our services? What are the business activities of resort hotels?*

- Introduction   introduce topic; background information; reasons for research
- Method   research questions; how research was carried out
- Findings/results   answers to research questions
- Discussion   issues arising from findings; limitations of research
- Conclusion   summary of main findings; implications; recommendations; possibilities for further research

Writing introductions and conclusions

Introduction

- Introduce the topic of the report.
- Say why the topic is important.
- Give background information.
- Give an outline of the report plan.

Note: No substantial information; this belongs in the body of the report.

Conclusion

- Summarize the main points in the report without repeating unnecessarily.
- Make some concluding comments such as likely implications or recommendations.

Note: No new information; all the main points should be in the body of the report.

Deciding when to quote and when to paraphrase

When referring to sources, you will need to decide whether to quote directly or to paraphrase/summarize.

- **Quote** when the writer's words are special or show a particularly clever use of language. This is often the case with strongly stated *definitions* or *opinions*.
- **Paraphrase**/summarize descriptions and factual information.

Incorporating quotations

- Use an introductory verb.
- Don't forget the quotation marks.
- Make the quote fit the grammar of the sentence.
- Show any missing words with '…'.
- Copy the original words exactly.
- Add emphasis with italics and write [italics added].

Additional material
5.3 Symbols and abbreviations for notes

Symbols

&, +	and, plus
−	less, minus
±	plus or minus
=	is, equals, is the same as
≈	is approximately equivalent to
≠	is not, is not the same as, doesn't mean, does not equal, is different from
>	is greater than, is more than, is over
<	is less than
→	gives, produces, leads to, results in
←	is given by, is produced by, results from, comes from
↑	rises, increases, grows
↓	falls, decreases, declines
"	ditto (repeats text immediately above)
∴	therefore, so
∵	because, as, since
≅	at
C	century, as in 20th C
§	paragraph
#	number, as in #1
?	this is doubtful

Abbreviations

e.g.	for example
c.	approximately, as in c.1900
cf.	compare
Ch.	chapter
ed./eds.	editor(s)
et al.	and the other people (used when referring to a book with more than two authors)
etc.	and all the rest
ff.	and the following as in p.10ff.
fig.	figure (used when giving a title to a drawing or table)
i.e.	that is, that means, in other words
ibid.	in the same place in the source already mentioned
NB	important
No., no.	number
op. cit.	in the source already mentioned
p.	page
pp.	pages, as in pp.1–10
re.	concerning
ref.	with reference to
viz.	namely
vol.	volume

5.4 **Student D**	4 Qualitative ≠ numbers; usually verbal info; used to find out attitudes, beliefs, etc. Methods inc. interviews, focus groups, etc. + reveal unknown probs; basis for quant. methods - in groups, opinions easily led by one person; only small numbers ∴ difficult to generalize

5.4 **Student B**	2 Primary = new info: from (1) people, e.g., customers, retailers; (2) observation, e.g., of shoppers + info = recent; can ask specific questions (good method for psych. research) - expensive; time-consuming

5.4 Student A	1 <u>Secondary</u>
	= info from sources, e.g., books, Internet, trade mags, reports, etc. (i.e., already exists)
	+ cheap; good overview of market; based on real sales statistics; relatively fast
	- reports → sometimes expensive; poss. out of date

12.4 Report B	**Findings**
	Key findings are as follows. Firstly, all three of the companies studied have several features in common: they are all luxury resort hotels in areas of natural beauty. They all emphasize that they use the latest technology, both for customer information systems and marketing. They have a strong focus on customer service.
	Secondly, there are a few differences between the three companies. Hideaway has diversified into other areas such as on-site catering and events services. It has also gone into joint ventures with companies in Europe. Paradise has been active in the USA where it has recently bought up an IT company and has become involved in virtual tourism. Just4You is providing health services (a spa resort) and has created an online community for its customers.

5.4 Student C	3 <u>Quantitative</u>
	= statistical info, usually thro' questionnaires
	+ good for factual info; overview of trends ∴ large nos.
	- sample must be v. big; people lie ∴ results may ≠ reliable; low response rate for questionnaires

9.4 Role cards

Role card 1 Harulang tribe

Wants: to provide eco-tours to tourists

Needs: transport, infrastructure

Offers: to provide art for public buildings

Role card 2 International hotel group

Wants: permission to build hotels/spa resort

Needs: airport extension

Offers: investment in infrastructure

Role card 3 Local government

Wants: foreign income

Needs: permission for hotel group

Offers: subsidies for tourism initiatives

Role card 4 Consultant

Wants: eco-tourism and education

Needs: government support/investment

Offers: a tourism development plan

Role card 5 Local retailer

Wants: tourist income

Needs: new shopping centre

Offers: investment in retail development

Role card 6 Chair of seminar

Your role is to chair the meeting. You must ensure that the seminar runs smoothly, everybody gets to talk and some sort of agreement is reached at the end.

11.2 Model Cornell notes

Review	Notes
	1 Political factors: e.g., taxation policies, pressure groups, election results, protection thro' tariffs or quotas, foreign companies coming into country
	(a) election results, e.g., Margaret Thatcher's new government 1979 UK $\longrightarrow$ mid-1980s privatization
	$\longrightarrow$ new business opportunities esp. service sector incl. tourism
	$\longrightarrow$ manufacturing declined
	$\longrightarrow$ policy copied by other countries
	(b) pressure groups, e.g.,
	Greenpeace (environment) $\longrightarrow$ Shell 1995 lost 50% sales
	Other Greenpeace campaigns relating to tourism:
	$\longrightarrow$ Iceland anti-whaling protest
	$\longrightarrow$ expansion Heathrow
	$\longrightarrow$ park development
	Tourism industry = maximize profit
	$\longleftarrow \longrightarrow$ sustainable tourism: bottom-line = $$$!
	InterContinental Hotels $\longrightarrow$ environmental audit major hotels
	Forte, Hilton, Holiday Inn, Sheraton $\longrightarrow$ shared programme
	mass tour operators $\longrightarrow$ working together in UN project, but … ???
	2 Economic factors: e.g., changing importance of different business sectors. Drucker ('The New Society' 2001):
	• 1913: farm products = 70% of world trade. Now < $\frac{1}{5}$ of economic activity
	• developed countries:
	o = big $\downarrow$ in contribution by agriculture to GDP
	o also manufacturing decline $\longrightarrow$ $\uparrow$ in service industries
	• 'new' economies: reduce farming $\longrightarrow$ $\uparrow$ manufacturing AND services (e.g., India, China) $\longrightarrow$ competition with developed countries
	• ? will China / India, etc. $\longrightarrow$ dominate world economy instead of US?

Summary

Wordlist

Below is a selection of words from this book that will be of particular use to students of tourism and hospitality. Unit numbers are given for each one. Where a word has multiple parts of speech, the part of speech of the word as used in the unit is indicated.

	Unit		Unit		Unit
A		boutique hotel	12	corporate	6, 7, 10
accommodate	3	brand (n)	5	cost-effective	8
accommodation	1, 2	break (n)	2	cultural tourism	2
adaptable	4	budget (n)	2	culture clash	9
add value	7	budget travel	2, 9	custom	9
adopt	10	business plan	7	customer base	12
adventure tourism	2			customer loyalty	12
adventurous	2	**C**		customer	1
advertisement	1	campaign (n)	11		
advertising campaign	7	carbon footprint	11	**D**	
advertising	5, 8	carbon offset(ting)	11	data	12
advice	10	carbon trading	11	data analysis	5
agent of change	9	career development	4	decentralize	10
agritourism	2	cash flow	6, 7	decline (n and v)	5
amusement park	7	casino	3	decrease (n and v)	5
analyse	5	category	5	dedicated (adj)	4
appeal (n and v)	7	catering	4	demand (n and v)	7
attend	6	celebrate	6	demographic	11
attendance	6	celebration	6	design (n and v)	7
attitude	4	challenge (n)	4	destination planning	9
attract	7, 8	charge (n and v)	3	destination	1
attraction	4	check in (v)	1	developing country	9
availability	6	check-in (n)	1	development	2
		chef	4	direct mail	8
B		climate change	11	disaster tourism	2
back-of-house	12	commercialization	9	dissatisfaction	1
backpacker	2	commitment	10	distribution channel	12
backpacking	2	community	9	diversification	12
beach resort	5	conservation	11	diversify	11
belief	9	consistency	8	diversity	9
benefit (n and v)	4, 7	construction	7	drop (n and v)	5
beverage	1	consultant	11		
blog (n)	12	consume	3	**E**	
book (v)	1	consumer spending	11	economic	11
boom (n)	2	consumer	3, 5	eco-resort	5
boost (v)	8	convention	6	ecotourism	2
bottom-up	10	core function	12	education	11

	Unit		Unit		Unit
marketing agent	4	preserve (v)	9	**S**	
marketing mix	5	pressure group	11	sales rep	4
marketing	5, 7	primary research	5, 12	sample (n and v)	5, 12
mass market	5	product	5	satisfaction	1, 4
mass travel	1	productivity	10	satisfy (demand)	5
medium-term	10	professional	5	scope	6
mega event	6	profit (n)	10	secondary research	5, 12
museum curator	4	promote	8	serve	3
		promotion	1, 5, 8	service	3
N		promotional	1	shoestring	2
niche market	5	protection	9	short-term	10
		purchase (v)	3	simulator	7
				ski resort	5
O				smart	2
objective (n)	8	**Q**		social	1
occupation	4	qualification	4	socio-economic status	5
one-off	6	qualitative research	3, 5	space tourism	2
operate	7	quantitative research	3, 5	special offer	5
operation	7	questionnaire	5, 12	sponsor (n and v)	6
operational	10			sponsorship	5
opportunity	4, 8	**R**		sports tourism	2
outlet	3, 8	real estate	3	stadium/stadia	3
outperform	5	receptionist	4	staff (n)	3
outsource	8	reconfirm	1	start-up (n)	10
overbook	1	recreation	1, 4	statistical	5
overnight	1	recruitment	4	statistics	5
overseas rep	4	recycling	11	stay (n and v)	1
		redundancy	4	strategic	10, 12
		region	1	strategy	5, 8, 12
P		regional	6	subsidized	3
package (holiday)	1	relaxation	1	survey (n and v)	5, 12
participant	6	renewable energy	11	sustainable	9, 11
participate	6	research (n and v)	3	SWOT analysis	12
peak (n and v)	6	reservation	1		
perception	8	resort (n)	2		
perform	10	resources	9	**T**	
performance management	4	retail (n)	7	tactical	10
performance-driven	10	retain	8	tangible	8
personality	4	ride (n)	7	target (n and v)	5
policy	9	rise (n and v)	5	technological	11
political	11	rise (v)	4	terminal (n)	3
pollution	11	rough(ing) it	2	theme park	3, 7
population	11				

Transcripts

Unit 1, Lesson 2, Exercise B 🎧 1.1

Part 1

Today we're going to talk about tourism. We'll look at why you study tourism. We'll also study the core theory of tourism, the basic theory, developed by researchers such as Leiper and Tribe. If we have time, we'll go into interdisciplinary studies that link tourism to other fields of study.

First of all, why do you study tourism? Probably, most of you will be studying tourism because you realize it's required to get a degree. Possibly, you feel it may be useful for a future career, or perhaps you're simply motivated because you've decided it's an interesting area of study. Tourism is certainly having a very great impact on our world.

This is something that Professor John Tribe recognizes when he writes that tourism is the world's biggest industry and it attracts undergraduates in ever-increasing numbers. He raises the very interesting point that because tourism has a large impact on the world, tourism courses need to show students what this impact is.

Unit 1, Lesson 2, Exercise C 🎧 1.2

Part 2

I'll just summarize for you this one paragraph from an article by Tribe – *The Philosophic Practitioner.* He says that the purpose of a course in tourism is to enable graduates to operate in their career. However, if we just focused on that alone, this would overlook an important feature of a big industry like tourism. Yes, it generates consumer satisfaction, employment and wealth; but tourism also leaves its imprint on the world in other ways. It creates an industrial landscape and causes changes to the social and economic relationships between people. When we develop tourism we create what you could call a tourism society. This society is made up not just of tourism-associated businesses, but of all individuals, communities, governments and the physical environments affected by tourism. So a special responsibility is placed on education to make people aware of the important role tourism plays.

Unit 1, Lesson 2, Exercise D 🎧 1.3

Part 3

Let's move on. What does 'tourism' mean? In a theory of tourism put forward by Professor Leiper in his book *Tourism Management*, it is defined as 'travelling away temporarily on overnight trips and visiting places for leisure-related purposes'. Leiper explains that there are a number of essential aspects to this definition, which I'll run through very briefly today.

To begin with, tourism involves travelling away from home and expecting to return to your usual residence. The second point is that you must spend at least one night away: it is, after all, a time when you're away from home. Thirdly, tourism involves a TGR, and fourthly a TDR. In other words, there is a place which the tourist comes from – the TGR or tourism generating region, and a destination – a place which the tourist goes to – the TDR, or tourism destination region. So if you live in London, then London is your TGR; if you live in Tokyo, then that is your TGR. That is where you would normally buy the resources that you require: you will buy your ticket there, you will buy your rucksack there; you will buy extra clothes; you will possibly even book hotels through an accommodation booking agency which, of course, gets paid for that service.

All right, the fourth point is that you would be visiting at least one, and possibly many more, tourist destinations. You might be taking just a single trip to one particular place; you might decide to go to Dubai and spend a week there; you might be doing a world tour, visiting many different places over a longer period of time. These are the destination regions, the TDRs.

A fifth and very crucial aspect of tourism is that, along the way, you will be travelling via a transit route – by plane, boat, train or any other mode of transport. This transit route may be the same for the way over as for the way back, or it may be different. And, as a tourist, you have an impact on the transit route – planes pollute the environment of countries they fly over, for instance; cars make noise; trains draw energy from valuable resources, etc.

So, in summary, you travel from home, for at least one night, prepare for your trip in your home area, travel to the tourist destination and use a route to get there, before you return home.

Unit 1, Lesson 2, Exercise E 🎧 1.4

Part 4

Travel is one aspect of tourism, but you don't go somewhere just to come back. Another important point, and this is the sixth aspect of Leiper's theory, is that you will engage in leisure-related experiences. These are non-obligatory – you don't have to do them. They are personally pleasurable, recreational or creative. You may, for instance, decide to go snorkelling, lounge on the beach, or have a massage. To a certain degree, tourism has to do with leisure, which is why we often see leisure incorporated into tourism courses, as well as hospitality.

Whether we're talking about travel, leisure or hospitality, all tourism shows the culture of the generating regions, and most tourism involves a cultural exchange in the destination region. This is aspect number seven. As a tourist, you engage with a different culture; you're away from your own culture for a while. This gives rise to a lot of interesting theories about cultural exchange, learning more about yourself, and learning more about the culture you go to. People often say that travel broadens the mind.

Unit 1, Lesson 2, Exercise F 🎧 1.5

Part 5

What other aspects of tourism and hospitality are there? Well, why do you go anywhere? You're motivated to travel somewhere based on information that you've received, one way or another, about the destination. You've received this information either prior to your trip in the generating region (for instance, by reading a book or looking on the Internet), or possibly on the transit route (at airports, for instance) or in the destination region, maybe at a tourist information office. So information is Leiper's eighth point.

The next point is that tourism involves change to your daily routine and activities. For a while, you experience a different way of life, a kind of time out, and you will be doing things that you may not normally do.

Leiper's tenth point is that, as a tourist, you expect that there will be a reasonable degree of security. You want the places you travel to to tolerate tourist visitors and, ideally, be hospitable. This is where the link with hospitality comes in. Hospitality is extremely important in tourism, because people need a sense of hospitality in order to feel comfortable in a place. Travelling can be quite stressful: you're in an unusual place, you don't know the people, and you may not know the language. There must be the sense that there is going to be a reasonable degree of personal security, otherwise people won't travel.

The next point concerns finances. As a tourist you will expect that your visit is going to be economically feasible, and that the activity will be worth the money spent – otherwise you wouldn't have embarked on the journey in the first place.

The final aspect is that tourists depend on the tourism industries, like hotels, accommodation providers, and the food and beverage industry. This is a bit of a grey area. Supermarkets, for instance, are not specifically aiming to foster or support tourism, but still many tourists rely on them.

So this is the end of your journey. You've travelled from home – your TGR – and you've spent at least one night away – your TDR. You've travelled to your destination via a transit route. You've participated in leisure activities, experienced a different culture and a different daily routine. You've received information about your destination, either at home or on arrival. You've felt safe, secure and welcome. You feel that your money was well spent. You've used tourist facilities and hospitality businesses, before finally returning home.

Unit 1, Lesson 3, Exercise E 🎧 1.6

Introduction 1

Today I'm going to talk about tourism. Somebody once said: 'The tourism industry produces expectations, sells dreams and provides memories.' I'd like to define tourism as travel for the purpose of recreation, and the provision of services for this. So, you travel somewhere and other people make sure that you can travel and enjoy your stay in your destination.

Introduction 2

This week we're going to talk about a historical example of tourism: the Grand Tour. We're going to look at who went on a Grand Tour, why they went, and where they went. I suppose you could compare the Grand Tour to what we now call a gap year: many of you may have spent a year abroad before studying here. The difference is probably that most of you will have had to work hard and earn a living while you were away to be able to stay away that long.

Introduction 3

In today's lecture we're going to have a look at how a holiday or leisure experience actually works. Even though you may be unaware of this, you take a number of recognizable steps to prepare for your experience in the months before you actually travel. First, and this can be as long as a year before the event, you decide where you want to go and what you want to do. Then you take a few weeks, or maybe months, planning. You prepare for your trip. Then you travel, you experience, you communicate, and finally you travel home and you tell everybody about it. It's not something you can pin down to a certain time-scale, but one step follows another, so let's look at each step in turn.

Introduction 4

Let's have a closer look today at mass travel. This is something we've all experienced, right? First of all, what actually boosted the development of mass tourism? We'll look at two important factors. Secondly, what was mass travel like in the early years? We'll talk about one of the first examples. Thirdly, what are the target groups for mass travel? We'll look at how these have changed over the years.

Introduction 5

This week we're going to be talking about the UK tourist market. What kind of market is this? How successful is it? The figures are amazing. Tourism and hospitality is one of the largest industries in the UK, worth approximately £74 billion. It accounts for 4.5% of GDP and employs 2.1 million people. There are, in fact, more jobs in tourism than in, say, construction or transport. Let's have a look at some more facts and figures.

Introduction 6

When you study tourism and hospitality, space tourism is perhaps not the first thing that comes to mind. After all, this kind of tourism involves travelling into space, staying in a space hotel and taking day trips to look at stars and planets. Does this all seem a bit far-fetched to you? Don't forget that the first commercial space flights are no longer just ideas on paper. In recent years, interest in the possibilities of space tourism has grown. The international business community and the media have become very interested in space pioneers like Virgin's Richard Branson.

We're going to start off today by taking a brief look at the history of space travel, and some of the more significant steps towards space tourism. So let's travel through time … from the initial enthusiasm for space travel in the 1950s to more recent plans for a space hotel.

Unit 1, Lesson 4, Exercise D 🎧 1.7

Lecture 1

A tourist, according to the World Tourism Organization, a United Nations body, is someone who travels at least 80 kilometres from home for the purpose of recreation.

A wider definition is that tourism is a service industry. It covers a number of tangible and intangible aspects. The tangible aspects are transport systems: air, rail, road, water and now, space. Other examples are hospitality services: accommodation, foods and beverages, tours, souvenirs. And then there are services such as banking, insurance and security. Examples of intangible elements are rest and relaxation, culture, escape, adventure. These are the things you experience. The intangible aspects of tourism are perhaps even more important than the tangible ones.

Unit 1, Lesson 4, Exercise D 🎧 1.8

Lecture 2

The word *tour* was introduced in the 18th century, when the Grand Tour of Europe became part of the upbringing of educated and wealthy British people. Grand Tours were taken especially by young men to 'complete' their education. They travelled all over Europe to places of cultural and natural interest, such as Rome, Tuscany, and the Alps. They went to see great buildings or works of art; to learn new languages, or to try new cuisine.

The Grand Tour was very important for the British nobility. They often used it to collect art treasures. This explains why many private and public collections in Britain today are so rich. Tourism in those days was mainly a cultural activity undertaken by the wealthy. You could say that these first tourists, through undertaking their Grand Tour, were more travellers than tourists.

Unit 1, Lesson 4, Exercise D 🎧 1.9

Lecture 3

First of all, you take a decision to travel. You may go to a travel agency. Alternatively, you may book a trip through the Internet. Having done so, you can start planning and preparing for what to do and see on your trip.

The information you acquire can come from a diverse range of sources. Often people have heard about a popular destination through hearsay; but they may also have done Internet research, or read books from the library. Advertisements in the media also help because they often allow you to send for brochures.

Having reached the destination region, you visit the sights. You could possibly take organized tours. While you go about the business of travel and leisure, you may want to keep a diary and visit the local Internet café to update your web log and send e-mails. And no doubt you may wish to make the occasional phone call to friends and relatives to tell them what they are missing out on …

On return you'll relive the experience by telling others of your adventure, sharing stories and photographs, and giving people souvenirs.

Unit 1, Lesson 4, Exercise D 🎧 1.10

Lecture 4

OK. So. Factors in the growth of mass travel. Well, there were two particularly important factors. Firstly, there were improvements in technology. Boats and trains enabled more and more people to travel to tourist destinations in the course of the 19th century; in the 20th century, planes made the sky the limit, literally. Secondly, there was an increase in people's spare time.

So what were some early examples of mass tourism? You may have heard the name Thomas Cook. Actually, his name is used by a well-known British travel agent. Mr Cook can be held 'responsible' for organizing the first package trip in history. In 1841 he took a group of people from Leicester to Loughborough by train. These cities were quite far apart, relatively speaking, for those days, so for most travellers this must have been a great adventure. You could say with some justification that this was the start of mass tourism as we know it today.

Who were the target groups for mass travel? The Victorians liked to travel, even though in the second half of the 19th century travel was only within the reach of the upper classes, of course, and the developing middle classes – people like merchants, traders and shopkeepers. In the 20th century more and more people earned higher incomes, planes were introduced, and travel became cheaper – within reach of most people in developed countries by the end of the century.

In our 21st century society, where most people have more spare time that they know what to do with, mass travel has taken on incredible proportions. It may be difficult now to appreciate that less than 150 years ago not that many people could actually take time off work to travel, and only a few people could afford transport, accommodation and time spent away from work.

Unit 1, Lesson 4, Exercise D 🎧 1.11

Lecture 5

UK tourism has been growing over the last decade, caused by greater mobility and the Internet. Last year overseas tourists spent £11 billion in the UK when they visited. Now this looks like a lot of money until you realize that domestic tourists spent £26 billion on trips of one night or more and a further £33 billion on day trips.

The UK ranks seventh in the international tourism earnings league behind the USA, Spain, France, Italy, China and Germany. The top five overseas markets for the UK last year were the USA, France, Germany, the Irish Republic and the Netherlands.

It can sound somewhat strange when you look at numbers. For instance, did you know that last year UK residents took 101 million vacations of one night or more, 23 million overnight business trips and 37 million overnight trips to friends and relatives?

Unit 1, Lesson 4, Exercise D 🎧 1.12

Lecture 6

After the Second World War, in the 1950s, there was a lot of interest in rocket designs, space stations and moon bases. But as Cold War tensions grew, the focus was increasingly on the 'space race' between the USA and the Soviet Union, which ended with the first moon landing.

It wasn't until 1985 that a passenger spacecraft was designed, called Phoenix. In the US, a travel company called Society Expeditions started 'Project Space Voyage'. They were offering short trips into

Earth orbit in Phoenix for 'only' 50,000 US dollars. They managed to get a few hundred people interested and collected deposits in the US, Europe and Japan, but in the end there wasn't enough investment to develop Phoenix further.

As we come closer to our own time, developments start to speed up. Shimizu Corporation, a major global construction company, chose to forget about how to actually get into space, but designed a space hotel in 1989.

A few years later, in 1993, the first market research survey on space tourism was carried out. More than 3,000 people in Japan filled in a questionnaire. If it showed one thing, it was that the concept of space travel was extremely popular in that country.

Five years later, in 1998, the 'X Prize' was announced. This was a $10,000,000 prize for the first person to launch a reusable manned spacecraft into space twice within a two-week period. At a press conference held by NASA, Mr Goldin, administrator of NASA at the time, said: 'I hope my grandson, who is two years old, will be able to go on a trip to a lunar hotel.' A few years before that, nobody could have imagined such a speech. From that time on, space tourism became accepted by 'real' space industry people. Burt Rutan and SpaceShipOne won the X Prize in October 2004.

In 2001, Dennis Tito became the first paying space tourist. He travelled on board a Russian Soyuz rocket bound for Space Station Alpha. He enjoyed a few days there and returned safely after eight days.

In 2004, Richard Branson of multinational company Virgin presented Virgin Galactic's plans to build a hotel in space and undertake regular space travel. Tickets were sold for a mere $200,000.

In 2007 NASA and Branson's Virgin Galactic announced they would collaborate in future manned spaceflight technology, and in 2008 construction of the first space terminal started in New Mexico.

Unit 3, Lesson 1, Exercise B 🎧 1.13

A restaurant purchases food, which it prepares, cooks and serves to customers who consume it on site. The prices reflect the investment in the real estate, the equipment – the kitchen equipment, tables, chairs, crockery, cutlery, and so on, and the staff – the chefs, waiters and other staff.

Unit 3, Lesson 2, Exercise B 🎧 1.14

Part 1

Today, we're going to talk about hospitality research. It's a fairly new research area, but as hospitality represents a huge share of the economies of many countries in the world, it's worthwhile looking into it. Did you know that last year expenditure on travel and tourism exceeded 6 trillion US dollars globally, according to the WTTC, the World Travel and Tourism Council? You can imagine that hospitality represents a large share of that.

During this lecture, you will see that hospitality has been the subject of much academic research and debate over the past 20 years or so.

First, we'll briefly look at what it actually means to be hospitable.

Then we'll consider the history of hospitality research over the past 20 years. We'll look at the most important researchers of the past and present, and we'll study the most important theories and approaches or methods they've come up with. Even though, as I just indicated, tourism and hospitality are closely linked, we will not focus on tourism really this time round.

Unit 3, Lesson 2, Exercise C 🎧 1.15

Part 2

Hospitality has been defined as two very different things. In general terms, it is seen as being hospitable, as the reception and entertainment of guests, visitors, or strangers, with goodwill. Needless to say, hospitality also refers to the hospitality industry: hotels, restaurants, casinos, resorts, clubs and any place or service that deals with tourists and making them feel at home. You could simply define hospitality as 'providing accommodation, food and drink', as some researchers do, but as Paul Slattery writes in his article 'Finding the Hospitality Industry': 'Hospitality customers not only buy products, but also facilities and services.'

Let's look at a restaurant, for instance, he says. 'A restaurant purchases food, which it prepares and cooks; it serves meals to customers who consume them on site. The prices reflect the investment in the real estate, the kitchen equipment, the chefs, the waiters and other staff, the tables, chairs and the atmosphere by the use of light, sound, colours, art and design and also the form of service. The task for the restaurant is to identify the specific demands of the customers at any time, and to organize the technology and processes to deliver the products, facilities and services so that customers achieve their aims in the restaurant.' I'm sure you hadn't looked at going out for a meal in this way, right?

Unit 3, Lesson 2, Exercise D 🎧 1.16

Part 3

In the past two decades, hospitality has become the subject of much academic research. Based on research by Littlejohn in the 1990s, you could say there were two main approaches.

In the beginning, research was dominated by the natural and physical sciences, such as food science, technical equipment design or technical equipment testing. It was a very scientific type of research and, as you will see, very limited.

Another approach to research was the management approach. This took a much wider view. It looked at the balance between four areas. It studied the external environment: what's going on in the industry, what changes there are in legislation, government regulation, the state of the economy, etc. It studied human resources: the people in the industry, such as hospitality staff, but also issues like management and training. It studied the technical infrastructure: what you need to provide a service, such as front office integrated software packages, closed-circuit TV security systems, communication facilities, etc. And it studied management information systems: the software and data you need to make decisions which allow you to improve hospitality services, how to gather such data and what to do with it.

Unit 3, Lesson 2, Exercise E 🎧 1.17

Part 4

Now, how has this research developed since then, and what theories have come up in recent times? In the late 1990s, Taylor and Edgar reviewed the hospitality research debate, including all the work done by Littlejohn, and they suggested that there were three purposes to hospitality research.

The first purpose is to uncover and make sense of existing behaviour. What is happening in the industry, what's out there? The focus is discovery. This is essentially a positivist or scientific approach, a method that looks at facts, data, things that can be quantified, not feelings.

The second one is to discover new ways of managing within the hospitality industry. Here the focus is on management. This is a normative approach, which is in contrast to the scientific. Normative researchers are interested in what people think and feel about hospitality.

The third purpose is to enable hospitality faculties at colleges and universities to educate future practitioners – an educational approach.

What happened after that? Well, a breakthrough really came in 2000, when Lashley and Morrison published *In Search of Hospitality – Theoretical Perspectives and Debates*. They argued that there were three domains of hospitality: there was the social domain (what happens between people on social occasions that are public), the private domain (what happens on a private level within families when they receive guests) and the commercial domain (how companies organize things). And there are various ways of looking at these domains.

OK, that'll be enough for now. We'll continue the lecture from there after the break.

Unit 3, Lesson 3, Exercise A 🎧 1.18

1 accommo'dation
2 e'quipment
3 in'vestment
4 con'sume
5 a'ccommodate
6 enter'tainment
7 ca'sino
8 fa'cilities
9 associ'ation
10 'industry
11 'subsidized
12 'purchase

Unit 3, Lesson 4, Exercise B 🎧 1.19

Part 5

So, where does that lead us now? Having looked at the history of hospitality research, it's time to look at the present day. At the moment, there are five principal schools of thought when it comes to hospitality. When I say that, I realize that we do have to generalize a bit, of course, when talking about this. In practice, you will see that these approaches sometimes overlap. They are, after all, ways of looking at the same reality.

First, there's the hospitality science school. Studies

of this type include research into people's diet, their nutrition, ergonomics – or how they sit and stand, equipment performance, and so on. There have been research journals in hospitality that report on this type of research but more and more hospitality-related studies of this type are published in specialist journals such as the *British Food Journal*. Hospitality researchers don't tend to read these, but practitioners in hospitality do.

The second principal school of thought is the hospitality management school. It's a very popular one and it's based on what we call quantitative studies, in other words, things that can be measured: how often, how much, how long, how many and things like that. And they're often related to studies of hospitality marketing, or consumer behaviour. It's based largely in North America; the *Journal of Hospitality and Tourism Management* is a good example of this approach.

Unit 3, Lesson 4, Exercise C 🎧 1.20

Part 6

The third school of thought is hospitality studies, which uses qualitative, as well as quantitative, methods to look into what people feel about hospitality. Qualitative methods are those that allow people to find out not so much how often, or how much, but why, and what for, and what's the effect of it, and how do people feel about it, which, of course, is extremely important too in this industry. This school is based largely in the UK, and reflected in the *International Journal of Hotel Management* and a journal like *Tourism and Hospitality Research*.

The fourth school is the one that looks into hospitality experiences. This is a new and growing school of thought. It focuses on the relationships and interaction between people and the experiences they have when they enjoy hospitality. It emerged in the UK and, as I said, you can find out about it in Lashley and Morrison's book *In Search of Hospitality*.

Unit 3, Lesson 4, Exercise D 🎧 1.21

Part 7

The final approach is called hospitality systems theory and there are Canadian, UK and Australian academics who have contributed to this. Like the hospitality studies school, it uses a normative approach, but it also builds on a basic philosophy. What is that philosophy? According to this approach, everything that happens in hospitality is linked. Remember that in an earlier lecture we talked about TDRs and TGRs? Systems theory looks at things like that, but also at what happens in between – transport, the environment, people, technology, finance, everything. We see systems theory reflected in the work of Professor Neil Leiper in Australia.

So, there we are. These are the five most important approaches to hospitality research – the hospitality science school, the hospitality management school, hospitality studies, the hospitality experiences model and the hospitality systems theory. Next time, when we get together, we'll look at tourism and hospitality, and how they merged together. We'll also have a look at the systems thinking of Neil Leiper.

Unit 5, Lesson 2, Exercise B 🎧 1.22

Part 1

Good morning, everyone. This morning we're going to start on the topic of tourism marketing. I'm sure you've covered some general marketing in other lectures, so some of this will be familiar to you.

In this first talk I'm just going to give you an overview of a few key concepts, and then other aspects will be dealt with in the next few lectures. Also, in your seminars and assignments you'll be able to cover all the important points in more detail. So ... er ... let's see – yes – to start with, we need to consider firstly what marketing is. In other words, why do businesses engage in marketing? And secondly, why is marketing so important for tourism? After that, I'll talk about market research, because businesses – well, any business, not just businesses in the tourism and hospitality sector – need good information on which to base their marketing strategy. Part of this involves analysing markets. So then I'll discuss some basic characteristics of markets, and I'll finish by mentioning some different types of markets.

Unit 5, Lesson 2, Exercise D 🎧 1.23

Part 2

Well, what *is* marketing? We might define it as 'the process of identifying and targeting particular groups of people with the aim of selling them a product or a service'.

Actually, marketing is arguably *the* most important aspect of management. You can manage your staff and your production processes well, but if nobody buys your products your business will fail. So, it follows that marketing must ensure that a business can satisfy customers' needs and at the same time that it makes a profit. But what *are* the needs of customers? Of course, there are many products which people will always need, but really successful companies identify gaps in markets and create new markets with new products. What I mean is, they anticipate consumers' requirements. A good example of this is theme park resorts. Have a look at Slide 1. I don't think there are any surprises in this top ten. Most of you will be familiar with these names, I think?

Already, in 1952, Disney realized the appeal that lies in fairy tales and fantasy, and that people love coming together for an unusual experience. What was missing were places for people to stay. Disney theme parks and resorts are now extremely popular, which is not surprising, because they appeal to young and old. And there is a type of accommodation for everyone, from luxury apartments to family hotels. They have really studied and analysed what their customers want to get out of the experience. Because of that, they cater for everyone's wishes: there's something for everyone. With their resorts, Disney have tried to turn the ordinary into the extraordinary, and 'making dreams come true every day' has become central to their global strategy.

Unit 5, Lesson 2, Exercise E 🎧 1.24

Part 3

Anyway, er … to return to the main point – fundamentally, successful marketing is about having accurate data so that customers' needs can be met. So what is it that marketers need to know? Well, first, they must begin by analysing the market. For example, it's essential to identify basic characteristics of the market such as its size, and which companies are the market leaders; that is to say, we need to look at the share of the market which each company has. Naturally, it is the aim of all companies to become the market leader – or to have the top-selling brand in a particular field.

If we take the beach resort market in the US as an example – you can see the statistics on Slide 3. As you can see, in 2006 this market was worth around $12 billion per year, and in terms of sales, it had annual sales of more than 2 million resort vacations worldwide. And what's more, it has been getting bigger. Just look at the figures …

Before the 1970s, going on vacation was a simple matter. But these days, there's a huge variety and choice. There are different resort vacations for

men and women, families and singles, rich and not so rich people, different ages, and so on … Er … Where was I? Oh, yes. We also need to be clear about the type of market. One way to categorize the type of market is to think about whether the product is aimed at a mass market, like ski resort or beach resort vacations, for example. Or is it more suitable for a niche market – by that I mean a small part of a larger market. For example, vacations for people over 50 are a niche market inside the huge vacation market. In other words, is the product aimed at just one narrow category of customer?

Unit 5, Lesson 3, Exercise B 🎧 1.25

Part 4

So how does the marketer get the necessary information? By research, obviously. There are several ways to categorize market research. Let me see … one way is to distinguish between primary and secondary research. Another important distinction is between qualitative and quantitative research. However, … oh, dear … sadly, I see that we've run out of time. This means that I'll have to ask *you* to do some research. I'd like you to find out what is meant by the four types of research I've just mentioned, that is, primary and secondary research, and qualitative and quantitative research. We'll discuss what you've found out next time I see you.

Unit 5, Lesson 3, Exercise C 🎧 1.26

1 'seminar
2 'overview
3 as'signment
4 'strategy
5 character'istics
6 suc'cessful
7 an'ticipate
8 'analyse
9 'qualitative
10 i'dentify
11 'category
12 va'riety

Unit 5, Lesson 3, Exercise D 🎧 1.27

Actually, marketing is arguably the most important aspect of management.

So, it follows that marketing must ensure that a business can satisfy customers' needs.

What I mean is, they anticipate consumers' requirements.

Fundamentally, successful marketing is about having accurate data.

Anyway, er … to return to the main point, it's essential to identify basic characteristics of the market.

Naturally, it is the aim of all companies to become the market leader.

Unit 5, Lesson 4, Exercise B 🎧 1.28

Extract 1

LECTURER: Right, Leila and Majed, what did you find out about the segmentation of the eco-resort market?

LEILA: Well, first of all, we looked on the Internet to see what resorts there were.

MAJED: I love using the Internet!

Extract 2

LECTURER: And what else did you do?

LEILA: We talked to the manager of a tour operator who specializes in resorts. She was quite helpful.

MAJED: That's rubbish. She obviously didn't want to talk to us.

Extract 3

LECTURER: Can you give us an explanation of your market map?

LEILA: Well, yes, it has a vertical and a horizontal axis: children versus adults, and economy versus luxury. And as you can see, we've put some different eco-resort types on it.

LECTURER: What do the rest of you make of this? Evie, what about you?

EVIE: Well, erm … I'm not sure really.

Extract 4

LECTURER: Majed, can you explain how you decided where to place the different resorts on your map?

MAJED: Well, yes, it's based on what the tour operator told us.

JACK: So it's secondary.

Extract 5

LECTURER: What do you mean by 'secondary', Jack?

JACK: I mean it's an example of secondary research. They did two things – they asked someone for information and …

EVIE: Actually, that's primary.

Unit 5, Lesson 4, Exercise C 🎧 1.29

Extract 6

LECTURER: Let's go back to the market map for the moment to see how it can help with segmentation. First of all, tell us about the dimensions you chose.

LEILA: Well, the tour operator we talked to used price and age group as the main ways to distinguish their services. Didn't they, Majed?

MAJED: Absolutely. Those were really the only criteria they used. So that's why we chose them.

Extract 7

MAJED: In their brochure they put the product aiming at families with children next to the EcoDirect product which, according to the lady, is aimed at couples without children. What's quite important is that they put the EcoPlus product, aiming at wealthy, elderly people, on a different page of the brochure, in smaller type and with no photos.

JACK: Sorry, I don't follow. Could you possibly explain why that's important?

MAJED: Well, basically they're trying to aim for the mass market first, I think. They don't seem to be as interested in the EcoPlus market.

Extract 8

EVIE: I don't understand how travel agents know exactly which eco-holidays are suitable for which market.

LEILA: Well, the manager said that as a tour operator they give very specific information about their target markets to the agents. For example, they say that the EcoDirect holiday shouldn't really be offered to families with young children.

Extract 9

MAJED: Yes, they tell travel agents exactly about the ins and outs of each product, so agents can achieve maximum sales.

JACK: If I understand you correctly, you're saying that the travel operators supply their travel agents with information about how to market their products.

MAJED: Yes, that's right.

Extract 10

LECTURER: This is all very interesting, isn't it?

EVIE: Yes, but if we could just go back to the market map, the EcoKids programme is for families with children so it goes on the left, and it's in the cheap to middle price range, so it goes around the middle on the vertical axis.

LEILA: Correct!

Unit 7, Lesson 2, Exercise B 🎧 1.30

Part 1

Good morning, everyone. Do the names Disney World, SeaWorld, Movie World and Six Flags mean anything to you? I'm Craig Horton and I run a theme park. I was asked to talk about theme parks and tourism, and to show you how these businesses work. I'm sure many of you will have visited a theme park at some stage in your lives. People often consider amusement parks, also called theme parks, American inventions. However, amusement parks were first created in the 'old world'. Did you know that it was in 1853 that the first amusement park was opened in Copenhagen, Denmark? We've come a long way since then.

You probably won't be surprised to hear that theme parks need to appeal to families, often have a themed environment, almost always offer some form of free entertainment, such as musicians and performers, and provide a high standard of service. Plus there's the fact that they must offer enough activities to make the average visitor stay for, typically, five to seven hours.

What I'm going to talk about today is one of the core features of tourism: that is, attracting people and entertaining them. I would like to trace the process with you of developing a park from beginning to end. What I mean is, we'll be looking at how a tourism business, in this case a theme park, does what it does. Bearing in mind that, in a way, a theme park is like any other company, big or small, it will become clear that it has a production process that it needs to manage, and that this depends on many other parts of the operation. I mean, it's everything from doing the research, designing the park, financing, building the park, and running it. It's a continuous process. Getting the name of your park to the public is one of the most important steps to take, and we'll be taking a close look at that. Near the end, I'll be making some predictions about the future.

Theme parks are a service industry, and yet they are very much like any other manufacturing company. I agree, a theme park hasn't actually got an assembly line, but it does have to produce the same experience over and over again. Would you call that mass production?

Anyway, we'll look at that later on.

Unit 7, Lesson 2, Exercise C 🎧 1.31

Part 2

It was Walt Disney who came up with the idea of starting a theme park in the 1950s. As is commonly acknowledged, Disneyland in Anaheim, California, which opened in 1955, was the first real modern theme park. Since then, the theme park industry in the United States, Europe and Asia has grown dramatically. The industry is now a multi-billion dollar business. Dozens of new parks are built every year. We have a few large corporate owners, and you've probably heard of most of them: Disney, Six Flags, Universal Studios, SeaWorld and Paramount.

I've been told that, in previous lectures, you've become familiar with the life cycle of tourism activities. The process of setting up a theme park can be thought of as a similar process. As you have seen before, there are many steps to this process. The first stage of the development cycle is coming up with an original idea and understanding the economic feasibility of the project. Like a regular business, a theme park has a cash flow, and needs capital investment. Another term for this is drawing up the master plan. Many ideas fail and never get off the drawing board.

What follows are the other ingredients, and even though these stages often overlap, they do happen in a more or less fixed sequence: design, financing, construction, buying the rides and other equipment for the park, installing those rides and the equipment, and organizing the show facilities. And then, finally, there is the actual opening of the park and operating and expanding the park over time. Typically, it can take three to four years to get from the idea to opening the gates.

Unit 7, Lesson 2, Exercise E 🎧 1.32

Part 3

An important phase in theme park development is marketing. What do I mean by 'important phase'? Well, let's take a look at the brochure I've given you for the new Goldorama Theme Park in Bristol, UK. This will open in six months' time from now. Marketing is a key area which must begin well before you open a park. You need to develop public relations programmes, get group sales going, and advertise. As you can see, Goldorama is doing all that, so everybody already knows about the park before it has even opened its doors.

In terms of marketing, it's very important to add value. Add value for the visitors and for the company. The ingredients for making a theme park – location, rides, events, staff, catering, etcetera – create something much more than just a day's visit to an amusement park. They create an experience which visitors will remember for a long time.

Looking at it another way, when you run a theme park, you are in the business of keeping people happy. It's a funny business, hey? In financial terms, value can be added for the company. It's easy to calculate: the lower the cost of 'production', the higher the added value or profit can be. The happier people are, the quicker they'll come back or tell their friends.

The difference between a successful and an unsuccessful theme park lies not only in the choice of theme and the rides and events it offers. Say you don't pay enough attention to staffing. You'll soon find your customers are unhappy because there aren't enough people to pay attention to them. In fact, the point is that to a large extent the way in which the park is run makes or breaks it, and to run a park successfully, finance, marketing, sponsorship, sales, operations, entertainment, administration, personnel, maintenance and general services need to work together. In this way, theme parks keep on developing and offering attractions to people which make them return.

And don't forget: typically, people living or staying within one and a half to two hours from any park will account for 80 per cent of visitors. So there's a lot of work to do to also attract tourists from abroad and maximize their enjoyment.

Unit 7, Lesson 2, Exercise F 🎧 1.33

Part 4

Now … er … let's see … oh dear, I see we're running short of time … Maybe I should skip a few slides. On the other hand, perhaps I should just say something about some trends in amusement and theme park development. A lot of research has been done into this area and there are a few trends that stand out.

First of all, you can see that, in terms of life cycle, the amusement park market is mature. In such a market, a few big players will own most of the parks around the world. I've already mentioned companies like Disney and Paramount.

Secondly, there will always be the race for bigger and better parks. Examples of this are better facilities, faster rides, the highest rollercoaster and the latest technology. More and more parks offer visitors the benefits of technology: virtual reality shows, 3D cinema experiences, ride simulators …

An ageing population means that parks need to offer entertainment that suits older visitors, too, and not just kids. What's important to realize in developing your theme park is that it's the older people who are bringing their grandchildren along.

Finally, and this is more marketing than anything else, theme parks have to be media savvy. What's different from, say, 30 years ago, is that now they must be designed for television and should be able to serve as locations for filming, celebrity events, competitions and conferences. After all, TV exposure will make tourists aware of your park.

Now … oh dear, I was going to mention the relationship between theme parks and the environment. More and more people will travel to visit theme parks and … well, but … ah … I see that time is moving on. So instead, I'm going to …

Unit 7, Lesson 3, Exercise A 🎧 1.34

1 con'tinuous
2 re'source
3 in'gredient
4 'benefit
5 fi'nancial
6 simul'taneously
7 manu'facturing
8 'maximize
9 'calculate
10 'sequence
11 enter'tainment
12 popu'lation

Unit 7, Lesson 3, Exercise B 🎧 1.35

Part 5

I'm going to finish with some more comments about the future of theme parks. The development of a big theme park often creates a demand for other tourism and hospitality services such as hotels, restaurants and shops. This is especially true of a park aiming at tourists. Why is this? Well, it's simple, really – tourists have to stay somewhere, they need to eat and drink, and they want to shop. So, theme parks generate demand for motel and hotel accommodation, entertainment attractions, and commercial and retail development. The best example of this is, again, Walt Disney World in Florida. The whole park is some 28,000 acres, although the Magic Kingdom itself is not that big. It's only about 100 acres! But surrounding the site are many other tourism-related facilities, such as a golf course, a resort hotel and other types of accommodation, a retail centre and an entertainment village with cinemas, concert halls, restaurants and shops.

I'll finish by reviewing the key factors for successful development of theme parks. To sum up, then, the first factor is that you must have a clear vision of what you want to accomplish. In other words, you must know what you want. You need to know which theme, which rides, which shows, and which markets you want to focus on.

The second key success factor is that each step of the process requires careful planning. Let me put it another way. Without careful economic analysis, careful planning and careful management, it won't work and you won't draw tourists in. Theme parks may appear simple, but the fact of the matter is, they are highly complex businesses. Not to mention the fact that you must make each guest feel special and entertain them to the best of your ability, day in, day out.

OK … oh, I almost forgot to mention the research task. Er … your lecturer has given me a research task for you to do for next time. We would like you to choose a theme, a location, the design and an advertising campaign promoting a new theme park in your country. The campaign centres on the idea of fun and getting what you want when you want it. It needs to communicate three main ideas: the extreme rides, the family rides, and the entertainment. Your target group are visitors within a 90-minute drive time. Research which steps you should take, what the park should look like, and how you should communicate with your target visitor group. Good luck.

Unit 7, Lesson 4, Exercise B 🎧 1.36

Extract 1

Now, as we know, what's very important for the whole operation is the location of a theme park: it's one of the most important decisions that companies have to make. I asked you to look at the case of Goldorama, who have decided to establish a new park near Bristol in the south-west of the UK. Why are they doing this? They already have parks near several other big cities in the UK, including London and Birmingham, which are not so far away from Bristol. Also, there are many medium-sized competitors, like zoos and water parks, in the area. So, let's have some views.

Unit 7, Lesson 4, Exercises C and D 🎧 1.37

Extract 2

JACK: Well. I'd like to make two points. First, Bristol gives easy access to several popular tourist destinations.

LEILA: Can you expand on that, Jack?

JACK: Sure, Leila. Bristol is near Wales, and the south-west peninsula of the UK.

LEILA: So?

JACK: So the point is that both areas are famous for their beaches and natural beauty. Visitors to the park will want to extend their stay and see more of the UK.

LECTURER: OK. So, what's your second point, Jack?

JACK: I was coming to that! My second point is that Bristol is an important regional centre.

LEILA: Yes, but that's true for London, too. Even more so. I don't think it's a good idea to be so far away from London.

MAJED: Well, I don't agree with that, Leila, because from what I've read, there's huge potential for tourism based in or near Bristol.

EVIE: Sorry, but who are we talking about, exactly? People from the UK, or people flying into the UK from abroad? Goldorama must see enough opportunities here to make this investment.

LEILA: Yes, we need to be clear here. It must be both. Anyway, I'd just like to say that according to what I've read, in the case of a service industry, convenience for customers is a major factor in location.

EVIE: In what way?

LEILA: Well, if you can bring your service nearer to the customer, you can charge a bit more. Also, you may be able at the same time to offer a more attractive service than the competitors.

EVIE: I don't get that. How can it be more attractive if it's more expensive?

LEILA: What I'm trying to say is, the company can charge more for their product but actually the customer might get the product more cheaply overall.

EVIE: I still don't understand. Can you give me an example, Leila?

LEILA: OK. Look at it this way. Theme park visitors typically come from no more than about an hour and a half away. People who live near Bristol would have to travel to London or Birmingham to get to the closest theme park. That would cost them time and money – say, £100 per person? If there is a theme park near Bristol they won't have to spend that money. If Goldorama charge, say, £25 more for the entry fee than London competitors do, the customers may still end up spending less. And what they don't spend on transport, they can spend in the retail areas of the theme park …

MAJED: So everybody wins! It's all about money, in fact.

LECTURER: Absolutely. In making a decision on location, companies have to think about their fixed and variable costs, as well as the income they are likely to get from a particular site. There are other factors, of course, and we'll come on to these later.

MAJED: Yes, and I'd just like to say something else. As I mentioned before, there are potentially a lot of tourists who might come to this park. So it's a good investment, as visitor numbers are likely to increase in the future.

Unit 9, Lesson 2, Exercise B 🎧 2.1

Part 1

Good morning, everyone. I'm going to talk to you this morning about the impact of tourism on culture. You will agree with me that each of the countries you are from has its own unique culture. Some of you may be from developing countries that are very keen to develop their natural and cultural resources. Others will be from countries that have a well-developed tourism sector already. Today, we will be looking at tourism in developing countries.

But before we begin I have a story to tell you. In this lecture, I'll talk about an imaginary country opening its doors to tourism for the first time and

I will outline some of the major consequences of the influx of tourists. I'll also give you a summary of possible solutions at the end.

It's a story of mismanagement and chaos. Every year thousands of tourists visit the capital city of this small country, which in the past was closed off to mainstream tourism. Realistically, the country can only just support its own largely agricultural society.

I'm sure you can imagine the large numbers of hotel operators trying to attract tourists as they greet them at the airport on arrival; you can see the noisy and polluting cars, trucks, taxis, motorized rickshaws and buses carrying them away along overcrowded roads, through streets littered with garbage, to badly built hotels where street vendors keep pestering them to buy things they don't need. Does this sound familiar to you? The seriousness of these problems cannot be exaggerated.

Of the many agents of change in society, tourism seems to be one of the strongest. It is also one of the most controversial. Of course, the point of the story is that it's really very dangerous for tourism operators not to pay attention to the culture of a country. I admit, there are not many undiscovered countries anymore, but there are still plenty of small and faraway places that are not prepared for discovery, and do not even have basic infrastructure.

OK, so how should we look at this? To start with we might make a distinction between two different types of impact on a new tourist destination. On the one hand, there is the impact of tourism as an *industry*. On the other, tourism and tourists themselves have an influence on the *people* living there. It's the first of these points that I'm going to focus on now, but it's worth pointing out that, in terms of effect, both are equally important.

So, to get back to the main part of my lecture … there are – as we will see – ways to help countries like these to manage and control their tourism growth. However, when you look at the tourism industry, you see that governments and foreign tourist operators often overlook a number of important issues.

Firstly – and let's continue, for a moment, to study our imaginary country – during the past few decades, there has been very little planning and investment in things like public health, electricity, drinking water, and last but not least, training local people for the tourism sector. But millions of dollars have been spent on publicity abroad to attract more tourists from richer countries. So, they are using scarce financial resources to promote tourism that is not sustainable at all. Which issues are playing a role here?

From the point of view of tourism management, there seems to be a 'use-and-discard' policy. You open up a region and, when tourists have left, you just open up a new one. As a result, a country eats into its own resources. As we will see, people are often neither educated about the needs and tastes of tourists nor about tourism-related problems.

So just to recap for a moment: as we have seen, countries opening up for tourism often make fundamental mistakes in their drive to boost their national or regional economies. Investment focuses on attracting tourists, but not on building a tourist destination. It's true to say that this is not unique and happens all over the world.

Secondly, and this always happens when an area is already overflowing with tourists, considerable energy and resources are spent on so-called 'improvements'. These are 'quick-fix' changes to the environment that actually spoil the atmosphere of a place. We see modern, ugly, concrete tourist accommodation among beautiful traditional local houses. These probably cost twice as much to build as it would take to build a local house in local style with locally available materials. The tourism operator fails to realize that what he builds is a poor copy of cheap, tasteless accommodation which, in the countries where the tourists come from, is generally used by poorer people.

Thirdly, there is the influence tourists have on the local population. The difficulty is that different players in the market may have different aims. Some are worried about the visible impact of tourism (housing, traffic, retail development, and so on) while operators who are trying to build a business only see the profits ahead. What they often don't realize is that there are two things at stake and they can clash. One is about strengthening local culture, and the other is about the growth of consumption. In many cases, these two turn the country into an uneasy mix of traditional culture and (let's admit it) Westernized business models. Globalization has a lot to answer for …

Unit 9, Lesson 2, Exercise C 🎧 2.2

Part 2

Let's now turn to our imaginary country again. As we shall see, tourism development had a profound impact on it. It was opened to tourism in the 1970s, in the sense that it allowed international exposure. In terms of cultural change, it started to understand global developments beyond its own borders. There are aspects of tourism that had a positive effect on the country when it first opened up to tourists. But first, let's take a look at what attracted the tourists to the country in the first place.

Like many of the undiscovered places on our planet, our imaginary country was a difficult and inaccessible place, and therefore only those with a genuine interest in its people, culture and religion visited it. Hmm, this is interesting. I've just remembered a Tibetan proverb that says, … let me think: 'If a valley is reached by high passes, only the best of friends and the worst of enemies are its visitors.' There's certainly some truth in that, because that is what it was like at first. Only those who were really interested came to visit.

If we move on now to the second factor, we realize that timing was very important. It could be argued that in the seventies, many people in the West had become disillusioned with the price of economic growth. Environmental disasters, pollution and fears about nuclear power and weapons were having their effect on people. So when the first travellers came to our country, they were impressed by its natural and pollution-free condition. They were impressed by the lifestyle of its people. Research has shown that they were also impressed by the way people with limited resources were able to support their lives and their culture without damaging the environment.

And you know what else? It did the local population's self-confidence and cultural pride a lot of good. They realized that their way of life was meaningful to other people – people they had always been looking up to. So from the point of view of tourism development we need to remember that it was through tourism that they learnt about the environmental, social and emotional problems that were part of the Western consumerist lifestyle.

An important point about the relationship between tourism and culture is that in countries that are developing tourism, there is often a strong indigenous culture that has not yet been washed away by the tsunami of modernization.

For a while tourism actually makes this culture stronger. Increasingly, however, we find that this development is overturned as time goes by. People become hungry for money, and use a cheap, two-flights-a-day tourism strategy. This encourages people to come in their thousands and make the destination little more than a theme park.

It's not surprising there is a real fear among people that this will affect the old culture. Tourism can have a negative effect on their way of life. Large numbers of tourists can undermine traditional beliefs, values and customs. In fact, there is a real risk of commercializing the very culture that they find so interesting. And where tourists are not sensitive to local traditions, their behaviour can cause great offence. To quote Professor Neil Leiper in his book *Tourism Management* (one of your core texts), 'relationships between tourists and locals are often shaped and damaged by stereotyped images that each part holds'.

It's true to say that the physical pollution of our environment can be prevented, but when the minds and the culture of a people are polluted, the effects can be long-lasting. So it should be clear that sensitivity to the cultural landscape is extremely important in the development of tourism.

So, what exactly have we looked at this morning so far? Well, to sum up, we have seen that in countries opening up to tourism, tourists are usually impressed with the lifestyle that the indigenous people lead. At the same time, the native population, often led by government policy or simply by greed, develops tourism activities without much care for the environment and the cultural heritage. If developments are positive to start with, these are often overturned and become negative.

Finally, and this is an interesting way of looking at the problem, we sometimes find that people focus on the wrong things. In fact, as Macleod points out in his article 'Cultural commodification and tourism: A very special relationship', in volume 6 of *Tourism, Culture and Communication*, published in 2006, it may be that policymakers and others are missing aspects of culture that could give advantage to certain regions and their local population.

Now I think that's all I'm going to say for the moment on the basics of tourism, culture and destination planning. Are there any questions so far? ... No? Good.

Oh, one last thing, perhaps ... to quote Mark Mann, from the *Community tourism guide*: 'Next time you go on holiday, ask yourself who owns your hotel or the airline or the tour agency who booked your holiday, or who supplied the drink with your dinner. Who is making money from your holiday? Much of what we spend on holiday – even in the developing world – ends up back in Western countries.'

Unit 9, Lesson 2, Exercise D 🎧 2.3

1 As we shall see, tourism development had a profound impact on it.

2 In terms of cultural change, it started to understand global developments beyond its own borders.

3 It could be argued that in the seventies, many people in the West had become disillusioned with the price of economic growth.

4 Research has shown that they were also impressed by the way people with limited resources were able to support their lives and their culture without damaging the environment.

5 Increasingly, however, we find that this development is overturned as time goes by.

6 It's true to say that the physical pollution of our environment can be prevented, but when the minds and the culture of a people are polluted, the effects can be long-lasting.

7 So it should be clear that sensitivity to the cultural landscape is extremely important in the development of tourism.

Unit 9, Lesson 3, Exercise A 🎧 2.4

1 'impact, 'influx, 'mainstream, pre'serve

2 ack'nowledge, 'consequence, 'heritage, 'influence

3 in'digenous, 'infrastructure, pub'licity, sus'tainable

4 'probably, 'generally, 'usually, fi'nancially

Unit 9, Lesson 3, Exercise C 🎧 2.5

Part 3

OK, let's turn to possible solutions to the challenge of dealing with culture in tourism. Now, it's important to remember here that globalization is happening all around us and the challenge of the preservation of cultural communities around the world is becoming harder. So what do countries need to do to stop the negative effects? … Well, let me give you a hint. Do the words *destination planning* mean anything to you now? Destination planning should be a national, regional or local community effort to plan tourism activities. It can make sure that the negative effects on a community or country are minimized.

By the way, I saw last week that some of you are using the Cornell note-taking system. That's very good. Do you all know about this? No? Right, well, if you want to know more about it, I suggest you look at *How to Study in College* by Walter Pauk, P-A-U-K, the 8th edition, published in 2004. It's very good, and it should be in the University Library. I'm sure that you all know the importance of taking good notes – and this system is particularly useful.

So, to get back to the topic: destination planning. Let's look at this idea in a bit more detail. Trying to make economic progress in traditional communities is essential but it's also very difficult. The problem is that people are using culture as the main tourist attraction. So they must create sustainable development to prevent the destruction of the community's identity. After all, not everybody is charmed by six-lane highways, global fast-food restaurants, high-rise hotels and coffee bars on every street corner.

But what exactly *is* culture then? Is it the beliefs of people in an area? Is it architecture? Is it nature? Is it the activities organized for tourists? Is it the regional or national cuisine? Is it a political system? Is it all of these? It's important that a destination planner takes into account the diversity of culture just because the term is very subjective. Even though the development of tourism is often about satisfying tourists' interests such as landscapes, seascapes, art, nature, traditions and ways of life, there is much more to a culture than meets the eye. One definition of culture given by thefreedictionary.com on the Web is: 'The totality of socially transmitted behaviour patterns, arts, beliefs, institutions, and all other products of human work and thought.'

What I'm going to say next may sound strange. When we look at tourism and culture, I believe that the quality of tourism depends on the cultural environment of the present, not on the cultural heritage of the past. What do I mean by that? I mean to say that tourism is developed and practised by people here and now, with present-day infrastructure, under present-day laws, with present-day means of transport, and so on. Therefore, I believe that to make sure that tourism operators develop responsible activities, policies need to be developed in cooperation with the community. There should, for instance, be strict regulation on the protection of the natural resources in a community.

Tourism operators and government should ensure that resources are conserved, and not abused. For example, tours to primitive communities in a certain area cannot be run by an endless number of operators, because the pressure on the environment and the community would become too large. Numbers of tourists in an area should be closely monitored, because if numbers are too high they put pressure on infrastructure such as roads, and on the natural environment.

OK, now, when I see you in tutorials, we'll look in more detail at all these issues. In the meantime, I'm going to set you a research task. Right, now listen carefully … your task is to find out about a particular tourism destination and the impact the development of the area has had, or is having, on the culture of the place. I'd like you to work in groups of four. Each group should report back on its findings.

Unit 9, Lesson 3, Exercise D 🎧 2.6

Extract 1

Tourism can have a negative effect on their way of life. Large numbers of tourists can undermine traditional beliefs, values and customs. In fact there is a real risk of commercializing the very culture that they find so interesting. And where tourists are not sensitive to local traditions their behaviour can cause great offence. To quote Professor Neil Leiper in his book *Tourism Management* (one of your core texts), 'relationships between tourists and locals are often shaped and damaged by stereotyped images that each part holds'.

Extract 2

In fact, as Macleod points out in his article 'Cultural Commodification and Tourism: A very special relationship', in volume 6 of *Tourism, Culture and Communication*, published in 2006, it may be that policymakers and others are missing aspects of culture that could give advantage to certain regions and their local population.

Extract 3

By the way, I saw last week that some of you are using the Cornell note-taking system. That's very good. Do you all know about this? No? Right, well, if you want to know more about it, I suggest you look at *How to Study in College* by Walter Pauk, P-A-U-K, the 8th edition, published in 2004. It's very good, and it should be in the University Library.

Extract 4

Even though the development of tourism is often about satisfying tourists' interests such as landscapes, seascapes, art, nature, traditions and ways of life, there is much more to a culture than meets the eye. One definition of culture given by thefreedictionary.com on the Web is: 'The totality of socially transmitted behaviour patterns, arts, beliefs, institutions, and all other products of human work and thought.'

Unit 9, Lesson 4, Exercise C 🎧 2.7

Extract 1

It seems quite clear that culture is a very important aspect of tourism. Whether you are an operator, a government or a local community, a knowledge of the destination's culture will help you to manage its development better. Let's look at two basic advantages that come from understanding local culture: firstly, you will appreciate the type of people the destination might appeal to; secondly, you will understand how the development of tourism will affect local people and, therefore, who needs to be involved in planning and decision-making.

Extract 2

… erm, I think one big problem is the fact that tourism leads to jobs that have very low status. This is very important. It is possible, we can see how is this very important … So let's look at the chart and … oh sorry, that's the wrong chart, just a minute … right, so here is some overview of the kinds of jobs in tourism … er, you can see, I think, this difference … do you have any questions about this chart?

Extract 3

… We could ask the question: how much does it cost to hire a consultant? Usually, this is very expensive but it is necessary because if you use a consultant you can get a good idea of what is possible and then you can let the community know how good your ideas are. A good consultant is also very important for the public because they can explain to a community what you are planning to do. Here we must look also at organizing meetings with locals.

Extract 4

So this is the main thing – culture is all-important in tourism. Why? Any area where you develop tourism has a culture. It doesn't matter what your definition of culture is: in terms of identity, all cultures are different anyway, which is what makes developing tourism so challenging. From the point of view of the local community, their desire is to improve their standard of living. At the same time, it's true to say that they don't want to give up their unique lifestyle. And as we shall see, the majority of tourists would like to experience something of that unique culture and compare it with their own. If we look at the chart I've prepared, we can see the main reasons why tourists travel. We could link this to the reasons why people want to develop tourism. Bearing in mind that you cannot develop tourism without building a good infrastructure, …

Unit 11, Lesson 2, Exercise B 🎧 2.8

Part 1

Good morning. My name is Dr William Grayson and I'm a business consultant. It's a pleasure to be here today as your guest speaker. My speciality is tourism and hospitality. I'm going to try to explain some of the major factors which exert pressure on the sector from the outside, that is to say, I shall mainly be looking at some of the different types of *external* influences which affect the way businesses in tourism and hospitality operate.

Don't misunderstand me, I don't want to imply that there are no *internal* questions for a company – as we all know, operators have to think about how they manage their businesses and their finance and so on. But there are also matters at a national and an international level which greatly influence decisions, and they're becoming increasingly important. To some degree, individual companies will be affected differently, but it is fair to say that they will all have to keep an eye on which way inflation or interest rates are going, or demand and competition in a particular location.

Not only that, but they also have to keep track of the government policies of the country or the countries where they operate and adapt and diversify wherever they need. In an attempt to try to keep the discussion of external pressures on business reasonably simple, though, I'm going to focus mainly on three areas: politics, economics and, very importantly, the environment.

Just to review something you've probably talked about in previous lectures. It's good to be aware that the best way to talk about tourism is to discuss it as a *system*. That way you can get a clearer picture of how the elements interact with each other and the surrounding environment. Do you remember the components? The five elements which form the tourism system are, one, tourists; two, TGRs (that's tourism generating regions); three, transit routes; four, TDRs (tourism destination regions); and, five, tourism industries.

Unit 11, Lesson 2, Exercise C 🎧 2.9

Part 2

To start with, then: the political influences on tourism and hospitality. Whether it's taxation policies, election results or pressure groups, politics has a crucial role to play. Governments often try to protect their country's businesses by signing up to a regional trading group which imposes tariffs or quotas. In the case of tourism, though, most countries will try to open up as much as they can; although I'm sure that some countries would rather have their own hotel chains establish themselves than have foreign multinationals dominate the market. Governments often encourage foreign companies and visitors to come into the country and visit sites and attractions or set up new operations and tourist venues such as hotels, theme parks and food chains. These things demonstrate the political dimension of business.

But let's take as an example the influence of election results. Historically, the UK is a good example of how a new government can bring about a major change affecting the business world in general. Let me take you back a few years, probably to before you were born. When Margaret Thatcher's Conservative government came to power in 1979, it started to address some of the difficulties of state-owned industries in both manufacturing and service sectors.

By the mid-1980s the process of privatization of state industries had begun to change the business landscape for ever. Many new business opportunities were created, particularly in the service sector, of which tourism is a major part. While manufacturing declined overall, it is clear that the business world in general, and tourism in particular, benefited greatly. These politically driven policies have since been copied all over the world.

Another area which we can include in the political domain is the effect of pressure groups. Governments and businesses have to deal with the political influence and public protests of these groups. No doubt you all know Greenpeace, who campaign on environmental issues: in 1995 their protests made Royal Dutch Shell seem so morally wrong that the company lost about 50% of their sales. Greenpeace are also well known for their protests and campaigns in the area of tourism. Do you remember their protests against Iceland's whaling industry (getting people to declare they wouldn't visit the country if Iceland didn't stop whaling), or against tourism in the Antarctic? Greenpeace is also part of a coalition campaigning to stop the expansion of London's Heathrow Airport. Greenpeace also works with scientists, public activists and authorities to develop parks and nature reserves with the aim of creating responsible, environmental tourism opportunities that don't do too much damage. We call this sustainable tourism. There are many other pressure groups which have been able to bring about major changes in public awareness of issues with either positive or negative consequences for business.

The funny thing is – well, I wouldn't want to call it funny, it's much more of a challenge – that at the centre of the whole debate about sustainable tourism are issues which the tourism industry finds hard or impossible to control. Why? Well, simply because they need to maximize profit. The hotel industry, for instance, is trying hard to encourage the responsible use of water and introduce waste and energy management through recycling, conservation and alternative energy. InterContinental Hotels was the first to start an environmental audit of its hotels, and in the end they produced an environmental manual for their hotels. Such guidelines have since been adopted into a broader programme which is supported by major hotel chains such as Forte, Hilton International, Holiday Inn Worldwide and Sheraton. There is a growing number of smaller and large tourism and hospitality businesses trying to do the right thing for the environment.

You need to wonder, though, whether these attitudes can have an effect on the mainstream. Mass tour operators are a case in point. Can we really convince these operators, who take the majority of tourists around the world, to prioritize environmental issues? The UN-led *Tour Operators' Initiative for Sustainable Tourism Development* is a positive step. However, critics of tour operators argue that they are always going to put their own interests first. The evidence shows that this is especially true with respect to airline carriers. In my view it will be incredibly hard to move them in the right direction. The effect of their unstoppable growth has been very harmful, in my opinion, especially from an environmental point of view. Their bottom line is market share and filling planes, isn't it?

Now, let's turn to economic influences on the world of business, including tourism and hospitality. An important economic dimension is the changing importance of different business sectors over a period of time. Peter Drucker, who was a major business thinker, gives a good description of this in his article entitled 'The New Society' published in *The Economist* in 2001. By the way, if you don't know anything about Drucker, a good introduction to his work can be found on a website at the University of Pennsylvania – I'll give you the URL later. Briefly, in *The Economist* article, Drucker explains how at the beginning of the 20th century (in 1913) farm products accounted for 70% of world trade, but farming has now fallen to less than one-fifth of the world's economic activity. In many developed countries the contribution by agriculture to their GDP has reduced dramatically. More recently also, manufacturing has seen a substantial decline in many of the developed nations. Manufacturing as an economic activity in many developed countries has given way to a major increase in service industries such as tourism and hospitality, with a consequent rise in the importance of finance and the money markets. These changes in the nature of economic output are, of course, reflected in the types of business which we find in these countries.

At the same time, in the newly emerging boom economies such as China, governments are trying hard to reduce people's reliance on farming in favour of new manufacturing and also tourism. India is another example of this: it has seen a boom in both these areas.

A thought to finish with is the question of to what extent these booming economies will become the main drivers of the global economy. One writer in *Money Management* magazine has no doubt that, and I quote, 'China will continue to be a dominant player driving world growth, which will have flow-through to other economies.' This could mean that we may see the older economies such as the United States losing out increasingly to China and India. In terms of tourism, we are likely to see improving facilities for tourists travelling to these countries, but also significant numbers of tourists from these countries travelling both within their own countries and to overseas tourist destinations. Now, I'm going to stop at this point …

Unit 11, Lesson 2, Exercise F 🎧 2.10

You need to wonder, though, whether these attitudes can have an effect on the mainstream. Mass tour operators are a case in point. Can we really convince these operators, who take the majority of tourists around the world, to prioritize environmental issues? The UN-led *Tour Operators' Initiative for Sustainable Tourism Development* is a positive step. However, critics of tour operators argue that they are always going to put their own interests first. The evidence shows that this is especially true with respect to airline carriers. In my view, it will be incredibly hard to move them in the right direction. The effect of their unstoppable growth has been very harmful, in my opinion, especially from an environmental point of view. Their bottom line is market share and filling planes, isn't it?

Unit 11, Lesson 2, Exercise G 🎧 2.11

1 I'm going to try to explain some of the major factors which exert pressure on the sector from the outside, that is to say, I shall mainly be looking at some of the different types of external influences which affect the way businesses in tourism and hospitality operate.

2 Don't misunderstand me, I don't want to imply that there are no internal questions for a company.

3 To some degree, individual companies will be affected differently.

4 … but it is fair to say that they will all have to keep an eye on which way inflation or interest rates are going, or demand and competition in a particular location.

5 Not only that, but they also have to keep track of the government policies of the country or the countries where they operate.

6 In an attempt to try to keep the discussion of external pressures on business reasonably simple, though, I'm going to focus mainly on three areas: politics, economics and, very importantly, the environment.

7 The evidence shows that this is especially true with respect to airline carriers.

8 Mass tour operators are a case in point.

9 Peter Drucker, who was a major business thinker, gives a good description of this in his article entitled 'The New Society' published in *The Economist* in 2001.

10 Briefly, in *The Economist* article, Drucker explains how at the beginning the 20th century (in 1913) farm products accounted for 70% of world trade.

11 One writer in *Money Management* magazine has no doubt that, and I quote, 'China will continue to be a dominant player driving world growth, which will have flow-through to other economies.'

Unit 11, Lesson 3, Exercise A 🎧 2.12

‚global 'warming

'waste dis‚posal

‚natural phe'nomena

'business oppor‚tunities

'threats to the en'vironment

in‚dustrial e'missions

en‚vironmental 'issues

a ‚positive corre'lation

'aspects such as pol'lution

Unit 11, Lesson 3, Exercise B 🎧 2.13

Part 3

Turning now to the issue of the effect of environmental issues on tourism … of course, a major concern is the problem of global warming. If it's as serious as some people claim, then it's likely to have a great many implications for tourism. Researchers like Braithwaite, Leiper and Witsel point out that not enough attention is paid to the transit route to tourism destinations. If destinations can be sustained, many people assume that tourism must be sustainable. But this assumption is rather misleading. We shouldn't forget the effect on transit routes – remember that component of the tourism system that I mentioned earlier – when deciding what impact tourism has on the environment.

So how serious a problem is global warming? First of all, there is no question that the Earth is heating up. We have to accept the evidence, such as the rise in temperatures, the melting of the polar ice-caps, the changing patterns in the habits of wildlife, and so on. But the real question is: is global warming the result of human activity? Some people claim, even some scientists have said, that it's nothing to do with humankind; it's the result of natural phenomena such as sunspots or volcano activity. But I'm afraid that just isn't true. It's quite clear that global warming is the direct result of human activity – especially business activity.

Within that, travel and tourism has a lot to answer for. Most of the research into global warming has concluded that the burning of fossil fuels is what is responsible. The evidence for this lies in the fact that there is a clear, positive correlation between the increase in the presence of CO_2 in the atmosphere and the rise in the Earth's temperature.

So if business is the cause, then business will have to be a part of the solution. Although some people may continue to claim that climate change is inevitable, what seems obvious is that business must play a key role trying to improve a dangerous situation – dangerous for the entire human race.

What's more, of course, we can see other threats to the environment from other aspects such as pollution, waste, and so on, many of which derive directly from the activities of tourism and hospitality. As everyone is aware, emissions from the airline industry or other forms of transport can damage both human and animal health as well as the environment generally. Waste disposal is becoming an ever more serious problem too. A lot of waste is generated by hotels, resorts, theme parks, festivals and so on. It's just not possible anymore to put all our garbage in a hole in the ground. Attitudes to waste – not just from industrial processes but also waste from the service industries – need to change radically.

When we look at environmental concerns such as these, the big question is how are we going to manage these problems? What strategies need to be put into place to help control CO_2 emissions, pollution and waste disposal? To some degree, as I've said, business must take responsibility for what is happening and must do something about it. This means ultimately that business and tourists must bear the costs of the changes that are necessary. Studies being carried out worldwide are looking at the 'footprint' we are leaving behind and what can be done to minimize it. In tourism and hospitality, for instance, a lot of research has been done into building environmentally friendly accommodation.

On the other hand, rather than being a threat, perhaps we should think about whether environmental issues actually offer business something positive too. Can tourism actually benefit from the steps which will be needed? We could argue that possible environmental solutions offer many opportunities. For example, environmental consultants can use their knowledge to advise operators; companies can develop environmental initiatives which appeal to consumers, ranging from environmentally friendly accommodation to restaurants serving only organic food. Other low-impact measures such as recycling may actually result in lower business costs.

Now I'm going to set you a task which will involve investigating some of the points I've raised. I want you to do some research into which areas of tourism and hospitality might actually be able to benefit from the changes which are going to be necessary for the environment. I want you to focus, firstly, on some of the new plans, methods and technologies for dealing with environmental problems, with respect to the environmental categories I've mentioned – global warming, pollution and waste – and in the context of tourism and hospitality. Secondly, I'd like you to think about whether these methods and plans to save the environment could actually benefit tourism businesses in the future or whether they will mainly affect them in a negative way.

Unit 11, Lesson 3, Exercise E 🎧 2.14

But the real question is: is global warming the result of human activity? Some people claim, even some scientists have said, that it's nothing to do with humankind; it's the result of natural phenomena such as sunspots or volcano activity. But I'm afraid that just isn't true. It's quite clear that global warming is the direct result of human activity – especially business activity. Within that, travel and tourism has a lot to answer for. Most of the research into global warming has concluded that the burning of fossil fuels is what is responsible. The evidence for this lies in the fact that there is a clear, positive correlation between the increase in the presence of CO_2 in the atmosphere and the rise in the Earth's temperature.

Unit 11, Lesson 4, Exercise E 🎧 2.15

Extract 1

The lecturer we listened to last week introduced a number of interesting issues. In my part of the seminar, I would like to build on what he said and talk about a number of new technologies which have recently been introduced as alternatives to fossil fuels: these include wind, wave and solar power. It's obvious that these depend to some extent on the climate and on where a country is located, but there is a lot of scope for development, although some people dislike the impact on the countryside of things like wind-farms. Hydroelectric power is also an important source that has been around for quite a long time in countries such as Norway, where they have a lot of snow and heavy rainfall. And, of course, there's also the idea of biofuels, which is anything based on vegetable matter, such as wood, corn, etc., which we can use for heating and to replace petrol. Just think of all the tourism opportunities this offers – a health resort could run completely on hydroelectric power or solar power or biofuels and people would not have to feel guilty about leaving their footprint …

Extract 2

OK, following on from what Majed has said, I'd like to mention some important environmental initiatives. You can see that as a result of global warming and because of worries about the environment, a new form of trading between companies has been created. This is usually called 'carbon trading'. Basically, what this means is that companies have an allowance for carbon emissions. If they create pollution beyond these emissions, that is, if they are heavy polluters, then they will have to buy 'carbon credits' from those companies who pollute less than their allowances. If they don't do this, they will face heavy penalties. This is what is known as the carbon 'trade'. So, what this means is that one company can be fined for creating pollution, while another may be rewarded if it reduces carbon emissions. The idea is to reduce overall production of greenhouse gases. Several trading systems already exist, the biggest of which is the one in the EU. The 'carbon market' is getting more popular in business circles as a way to manage climate change. You can imagine what this would do to global tour operators and airlines.

Extract 3

Right. Thank you, Evie. I'm going to expand on what Evie just said by mentioning another important initiative. What is usually called 'carbon offsetting' is similar in many ways to the concept of carbon trading. Carbon offsetting involves the calculation of your carbon footprint and then, depending on the result, the purchase of 'carbon offset credits'. Let me try and make this clearer with an example. For instance, if you travel a lot by plane then you might need to offset your carbon footprint (a concept developed by Wackernagel and Rees in 1995, by the way) by some more environmentally friendly green action such as reducing energy use in your house or not using your car so much. Several companies already exist to advise on this and to manage it: for example, carbonfootprint.com. So, in the context of tourism, airline companies, for instance, can be (and, in some countries, already are) forced to invest money in projects that undo (or try to undo) the damage they have caused. Operators will try to get some of this money back, of course, so if as a tourist you book a ticket online these days you will probably be asked whether you want to offset the distance you are flying by paying a little bit extra.

Extract 4

As well as carbon issues we can also look at a very different sort of initiative. Here, I'm going to explain about the concept and philosophy of zero waste. Zero waste has been around for a while; basically, it is a strategy which looks for inefficiencies in the way materials are produced, packaged, used and disposed of. In terms of tourism you will agree with me that there is an endless array of materials out there – just think of brochures, packaging, food waste, etc., etc. As well as community, home and school programmes for waste reduction, there are business and industrial opportunities, for example in the design of products, maximization of energy use, and improved efficiency methods. The aim is to remove the 'Take, Make, Waste' principle which we have at present and to replace it with the 'Waste Equals Resource' approach. This would help to remove all waste from the environment. So basically what we're saying in terms of tourism and hospitality is, I suppose, that facilities must be designed in harmony with the local environment; that design must be sustainable; that people should avoid using non-renewable energy sources; that people should only use renewable or recycled materials.